Health and Social Care

DIPLOMA LEVEL 3

Pat Ayling

Contributing authors:
Eleanor Langridge
Val Michie

D0192034

Text © Pat Ayling 2012
Original illustrations © Nelson Thornes Ltd 2012

Published in 2012 by:
Nelson Thornes Ltd
Delta Place
27 Bath Road
CHELTENHAM
GL53 7TH
United Kingdom

12 13 14 15 16 / 10 9 8 7 6 5 4 3 2 1

A catalogue record for this book is available from the British Library

ISBN 978 1 4085 1536 5

Cover photograph: © Agphotographer/fotolia
Illustrations by Angela Lumley and Peters and Zabransky UK Ltd
Page make-up by Fakenham Prepress Solutions, Norfolk
Printed and bound in Spain by GraphyCems

Photo acknowledgements
Alamy: © itanistock p61 (Sulamain); fotolia: © Maridav p7 (right); © CANDIDEYE p48; © Yuri Arcurs p49 (top left); © Monkey Business p61 (Sofia); © AVAVA p116; iStock: © Sarah Garner p1; © Ricahrd Foreman p7 (left); © Daniel Laflor p24; © digitalskillet p49 (top middle); © Ирина Бекулова p49 (top right); © Factoria Singular p49 (bottom left); © Andrew Parfenov p49 (bottom right); © ajijchan p61 (Meena); © Fred Froese p61 (Harry); © Mike Cherim p61 (Sam); © Chris Schmidt p66; © anne de Haas p79; © Rich Legg p100; © Michael Krinke p147; © rollover p179; © Ron Bailey p216; © sturti p237.

Contents

Introduction

Welcome to the Health and Social Care Level 3 Diploma Course Companion. It is a companion to support you throughout your course and record your progress.

This workbook-style book is designed to be used alongside **any** student book you are using. It is packed full of activities for you to complete in order to check your knowledge and reinforce the essential skills you need for this qualification.

Features of the Course Companion are:

Unit opener – this page contains a brief introduction to each unit along with the learning objectives you need to achieve.

Activities – a wide variety of learning activities are provided for you to complete in your Companion. Each activity is linked to one of the Personal, Learning and Thinking Skills to help you practise these fundamental skills:

– Reflective Learner

– Creative Thinker

– Teamworker

– Self Manager

– Independent Enquirer

– Effective Participator

You will also notice additional icons that appear on different activities, these link to the following core skills and also to employment rights and responsibilities in the workplace:

– Literacy

– ICT

– Employment, Rights and Responsibilities

Case studies – a range of real life examples of different scenarios to provide context to the topics covered. Case studies are also linked to one of the Personal, Learning and Thinking Skills and the core skills or employment rights and responsibilities in the workplace (where appropriate).

Key terms – during your course you'll come across new words or new terms that you may not have heard before, so definitions for these have been provided.

Assessor tip – tips and advice are provided by an experienced assessor to help you demonstrate competency and build your portfolio.

Your questions answered – your expert author, Pat Ayling, answers some burning questions you may have as you work through the units.

Are you ready for assessment? – at the end of each unit you will find a checklist of the skills and knowledge covered in the unit. If you're confident you have covered these, then you're ready for assessment!

Good luck!

UNIT SHC 31

Promote communication in health and social care settings

This unit provides you with the knowledge that will help you to communicate effectively with a range of different people, including young people, older people and those with disabilities, and with people of varying races, cultures and beliefs.

It addresses the different types of communication, from verbal, non-verbal and use of body language, to using the written word (such as email) and how to overcome barriers that may arise. It also addresses confidentiality issues, how to maintain confidentiality in your day-to-day work, and understanding how to report issues that are in breach of the rights of protection.

You will need to be able to:
- ✿ understand why effective communication is important in the work setting
- ✿ meet the communication and language needs, wishes and preferences of individuals
- ✿ overcome barriers to communication
- ✿ apply principles and practices relating to confidentiality.

Why effective communication is important in the work setting

The different reasons people communicate

We need to communicate with other people for all sorts of reasons: to ask for information, to give information and to express thoughts and feelings. Normally we think of communication as speaking to someone (verbal communication). However, we can also use other methods: some that do not use words and some that use words that are not spoken, such as writing a letter or using email.

It is often stated that it is not what we say but **how** we say it that is important. The power of **non-verbal communication (NVC)** and the use of **body language** and **gestures** can be enormous. If we are not careful we can give out the wrong messages with just a quick gesture or a frown! We must be ready to adjust our behaviour if we think we have given out a negative **cue.**

There will be activities to help you understand the power of non-verbal communication later in the unit.

Identify different reasons for communication in the sector

ACTIVITY

Think about the reasons for using different methods of communication in the health and social care sector. This activity gives you some tasks that may form part of your duties. Tick the methods of communication that you think apply when carrying out these tasks and give a specific example in the last column from a work setting. Also think about supporting verbal information; when might it be a good idea to reinforce or repeat what you have said in another form?

An example has been done for you.

Task	Verbal communication	Non-verbal communication	Written or electronic communication	Example from a setting
How to take medication.	✓	✓	✓	Explaining this to an individual requires spoken words. It may also involve a demonstration and some written instructions. You will also report on your actions and the individual's response.

Task	Verbal communication	Non-verbal communication	Written or electronic communication	Example from a setting
Building a positive relationship.				
Relaying messages.				
Reporting concerns.				

Why is it important?

In the care sector there are many important reasons to get communication just right. You can communicate with other staff or with patients or residents. It may be in a one-to-one situation, or in groups, for example when you are in a meeting.

It would be useful for you to research some theories of effective communication such as **Tuckman's theory of group formation** and **Argyle's theory of the communication cycle** (see page 5).

You should also maintain a positive regard for the person in your care – that is, to accept them as they are, whatever they say or do. This helps you to communicate without your feelings getting in the way.

key term

Tuckman's theory of group formation: a theory suggesting that teams develop in stages. This is the forming of a team, the storming process (such as discussions and plans), norming (plans are being put into place) and performing (the team works together).

Communication is one of the key ways in which we build and maintain relationships with others. The words we use, voice pitch and tone and body language are all ways in which we show others our genuineness, acceptance of them as individuals and empathy. These are important factors in relationships as through them we affirm the other person's worth and importance to us. This engenders trust, which lies at the foundation of any relationship.

ACTIVITY

Imagine this is your first day at work on a hospital unit. Look at the table below, which gives the reasons for **effective communication** at the top of each column.

Read the jumbled statements under the table and enter them into the correct column, but note that there are three inappropriate answers. You must cross these out.

You may find it useful to discuss this activity with a friend or colleague.

To seek information	To give information	To express feelings	To build relationships
Explain your duties to the patients.	Read policies.	Say 'I am quite nervous'.	Clarify your concerns.
Immediately make a drink.	Ask what is expected of you.	Say 'I don't want to clean up vomit'.	Greet each patient with a smile.
Introduce yourself to the manager.	Offer your help.	Go for an early lunch and return late.	Explain your experiences to the manager.
Make notes.	Give reassurance.	Ask questions.	Talk to the patients.

ACTIVITY

Much of the communication between you, as a worker, and the individuals you support will be based on building and maintaining a working relationship with each person. Listening and using empathy will be important aspects of this process. Think about the people you support and their relatives. Reflect on how you communicate with them and how this may be different to the way in which you communicate with colleagues.

List at least four ways in which you can communicate more effectively with service users and relatives.

✿

✿

✿

✿

key terms

Argyle's theory of the communication cycle: a theory suggesting that ideas are communicated, acted upon and reviewed. There are six stages but the hardest is the 'decoding' stage because that is when our messages are understood or misunderstood by others.

Effective communication: any method of communication that achieves the desired result, that is, so the individual can understand and express needs or respond correctly to instructions.

How poor communication skills can affect relationships

ACTIVITY

Indicate whether you think the statements below are true or false.

TRUE/FALSE

✿ To use non-verbal communication successfully, you need to be able to accurately read the cues from others and adapt your own behaviour.

✿ Facial expressions, such as anger and confusion, are universal – they are the same across all cultures.

✿ Gestures, such as hand waves and signals, are the same across all cultures.

✿ We must get closer to a person and touch them to show respect.

✿ Our posture can indicate how confident we are.

✿ Active listening means using no other means of verbal communication.

✿ Body language can easily be misinterpreted.

✿ Paraphrasing is to shout like a parrot.

Assessor tip

You could have a reflective discussion with your assessor to show your understanding of effective communication. Reflect on how you communicated in two different situations: one that went well and one that didn't go well. Think about how your verbal and non-verbal communication affected the outcome in each situation.

Meet the communication and language needs, wishes and preferences of individuals

Establish the communication wishes and preferences of individuals

Not everyone finds communicating with others easy. You will need to quickly establish how to best do this in order to give the appropriate care according to someone's preferences and wishes.

ACTIVITY

Read the examples of people for whom communication is difficult. For each person, choose two strategies from the list in the box on page 7, to demonstrate that you understand their difficulties and can help them to establish better communication channels. Give a reason for your choice.

Example of individual with communication difficulty	Two strategies to establish preferences for communicating	Give your reason
75-year-old woman speaks only Arabic.		
68-year-old man has sustained a stroke and has little speech.		
86-year-old woman has dementia and does not understand you.		
25-year-old woman has lost her sight.		
79 year-old man has a hearing impairment.		

Options
1. Ask the person how they would like to be addressed and identify their needs and wishes.
2. Arrange for a member of the family to visit to discuss strategies.
3. Arrange for the person to use picture sequence cards.
4. Show the person images of items in their setting for them to point at when they need them.
5. Use sign language.
6. Call in an English teacher.
7. Ask for advice from an interpreter.
8. Call a speech therapist for advice.
9. Ask them to write requests on paper.
10. Check the person understands by asking them to follow simple gestures.
11. Use positive non-verbal communication, such as touch.
12. Consult with the person's family and review what is working

Describe the factors to consider when promoting effective communication

Whenever you meet someone for the first time it is essential to promote effective communication. This means being positive in your interactions and having a positive regard for the individuals in your care. As we have seen in the previous activities, this is demonstrated by using non-verbal communication as well as positive verbal language.

It is important to consider environmental factors such as background noise, lighting quality and the level of privacy as these all affect the effectiveness of communication.

Positive body language

ACTIVITY

Look at the images below and describe the body language that you see. Explain how these signs show positive or negative cues.

A

I think Image A shows positive/ negative cues because

B

I think Image B shows positive/ negative cues because

Demonstrate a range of communication methods and styles to meet individual needs

When you meet someone for whose care you will be responsible, it is very important not only to gather information necessary for their care needs but to also build a positive and trusting relationship with them. As you have noted in the previous activities, we do not always use the same methods of communicating with people. We adjust our methods to suit the expressed needs and preferences of the individual.

Active listening is about more than just hearing what is being said. It is also about observing the individual, understanding the meaning behind their words, then combining this with their non-verbal communication. This will enable you to use appropriate questions and prompts to encourage the individual to express themselves. Active listening involves taking the time to fully concentrate on the individual. To be effective, this needs to be done face-to-face.

Communication styles

There are four main styles of communication. The following table outlines the main features of each style.

Communication Style	Main features
Assertive.	This is how we naturally express ourselves when we are confident and our self esteem is intact. It is the most effective and productive as we are able to communicate without hidden motives or by manipulating others. Using an assertive communication style shows we care about our relationships with others and work to achieve a win-win situation through clearly expressing our needs, recognising our limitations while being unwilling to be coerced into doing something against our will or best interests.
Aggressive.	This style always involves manipulating others to do what we want, for example through intimidation, anger or making them feel guilty. This style doesn't encourage healthy and equal relationships.
Passive.	This style of communication relies on the person complying (agreeing) with the wishes of other people. A person chooses to be passive to avoid confrontation as they feel uncomfortable in dealing with a certain type of situation. As a result the person communicates very little, having learnt it is safer to show little or no reaction.
Passive-aggressive.	This describes a combination of styles where the individual avoids confrontation (passive) but attempts to address the situation through manipulation (aggressive).

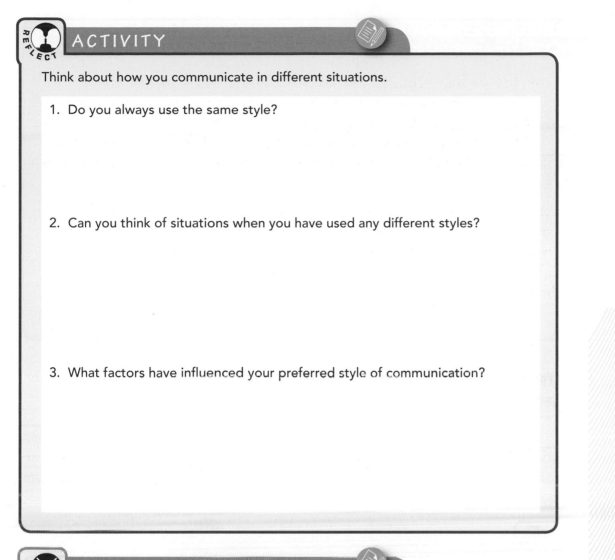

ACTIVITY

Think about how you communicate in different situations.

1. Do you always use the same style?

2. Can you think of situations when you have used any different styles?

3. What factors have influenced your preferred style of communication?

ACTIVITY

Think about the different ways in which you communicate with others at work. Complete the table by identifying two reasons for using a particular communication method, two benefits of using it and by giving two things to consider when using each method.

Communication method	Two reasons for use	Two benefits of use	Two things to consider
Face-to-face conversation.	1. 2.	1. 2.	1. 2.
Telephone conversation.	1. 2.	1. 2.	1. 2.

Communication method	Two reasons for use	Two benefits of use	Two things to consider
Written communication.	1.	1.	1.
	2.	2.	2.
Email or text.	1.	1.	1.
	2.	2.	2.

Demonstrate how to respond positively to different reactions

In order to have a selection of effective communication methods that you can use, you need to understand the individuals in your care. We have previously looked at identifying communication methods, but sometimes you will need to change them quickly depending on the reactions that you get.

ACTIVITY

Read the principles and the scenario below then judge for yourself if the principles were met. Place a cross at the points in the conversation where you think Khalid was not practising effective communication and write at least three points to demonstrate how he should have handled the interaction when meeting Mr Palm.

Principles

❁ Use open-ended and closed questions appropriately. Open-ended questions allow people to respond in as much detail as they wish. These questions often start with 'How', 'What', 'Where' and 'When'. Closed questions have a limited choice of answers, for example 'Yes' or 'No'.

❁ Use eye contact and encouraging gestures, such as leaning forward and nodding.

❁ Maintain an interest in the person, helping to build a positive relationship.

❁ Use active listening techniques such as paraphrasing.

❁ Summarise and gain permission to share care plan details with other staff.

Scenario and conversation

The carer, Khalid, is tired as he has worked too much overtime. His last duty of the day is to meet Mr Palm, who has just been admitted to the unit. On entering his room, he notices that Mr Palm is quite agitated and is a wheelchair user.

K: Hello, my name is Khalid and I need to take a few details from you.

Mr P: What did you say?

K: (raising voice) I need to take a few details from you.

Mr P: I'm afraid I am rather deaf.

K: Yes.

Mr P: (coming closer to K) Now, what is it you want?

K: Are you on medication?

Mr P: I take lots of tablets, yes.

K: Well, I need to know what you take.

Mr P: I never remember the names.

K: Have you brought them?

Mr P: I have not had time to find them, I've only just arrived, but I really need the toilet.

K: Yes, but can we just sort out your tablets?

1. Were any of the principles met?

2. In order to show effective communication I would have ...

   ✿

   ✿

   ✿

Overcome barriers to communication

How people from different backgrounds may use communication methods in different ways

You have noted different ways of using positive non-verbal communication to contribute to effective communication. However, some non-verbal communication can be interpreted differently according to culture and race.

Although you do not need to be aware of the full range of differences in body language and gestures, you do need to understand that, apart from facial expressions, body language varies between different cultures.

It is important for you to be aware of some basic differences so you do not misunderstand gestures from people who originate from other cultures. One example is the thumbs-up sign, which indicates 'all is good' in the UK but is a rude gesture in Arab countries.

Body language varies between different cultures

key term

Barriers to effective communication: anything that hinders effective communication, such as language, hearing impairments, visual impairments, inappropriate vocabulary, excessive background noise or poor lighting.

Many Asians would consider it inappropriate to touch someone on the head, as this is believed to be a sacred part of the body. In the Middle East the left hand is reserved for bodily hygiene and should not be used to touch another person or to transfer objects. Touch between men and women is considered inappropriate in Muslim cultures.

In Western cultures maintaining eye contact is considered to show the person is being attentive and listening. In Hispanic, Asian, Middle Eastern and Native American cultures, eye contact is thought to be disrespectful, and so a lack of eye contact would not be seen as indicating the person is not listening. In addition, in some cultures women may especially avoid eye contact with men, because it can be taken as a sign of sexual interest.

Identify barriers to effective communication and how to overcome them

The next activity highlights methods and resources that you need to know about in order to break down **barriers to effective communication**. Barriers may result from:

- environmental factors, for example noise
- the individual's stage of development
- ill health, distress or emotional difficulties
- sensory impairment or disability
- language or cultural differences
- unfamiliar language, for example slang.

ACTIVITY

Read the brief summaries of people needing care in the community and match the individual with the most appropriate strategy (given in the right-hand column) by drawing a line to match them up.

Individuals in the community	The most appropriate communication method
Following a stroke, Lee is unable to form words.	Symbol or picture cards that may be used in a sequence.
Ali has profound hearing loss and limited vision.	Suggest the learning of Braille.
Sanjay can no longer cope with his father, who has Alzheimer's disease.	Use written questions or statements with speech therapy.
Su-min has lost her sight following an accident.	Referral for specialist intervention and use sensory aids.
Anila has complex learning difficulties and cannot easily follow verbal or written instructions.	Assist with letter writing, use of a translator and refer to services.
Mina speaks little English and cannot read or write. She needs to contact the local council.	Allow plenty of time to sit and discuss all needs and options.

When considering ways to overcome barriers to communication, remember the simple solutions, such as reducing noise and interruptions, as well as the more complex solutions, such as advocacy or using language services.

Effective communication

ACTIVITY

The following words relate to negative and positive factors of effective communication. Tick the positive ones and circle the words in the grid. You could use two different colours to circle the positive and negative terms.

Y	M	D	I	A	L	E	C	T	S	V	C	A	A	J	D	W	I	F	G
Q	Z	V	K	Y	F	L	M	A	K	D	X	M	A	T	G	C	M	V	Z
X	R	S	I	G	N	I	N	G	A	C	H	B	N	F	Y	U	W	A	Z
I	E	T	J	A	I	A	O	N	P	D	E	J	C	I	Z	S	S	D	P
P	P	V	A	C	M	K	W	K	C	W	A	W	I	G	N	M	E	V	B
W	E	X	N	J	P	X	X	T	M	B	L	P	N	U	J	S	S	O	B
T	A	T	O	P	A	F	V	Q	R	W	T	G	D	R	Z	Y	D	C	U
L	T	R	Z	V	I	V	J	T	W	E	H	W	U	E	Z	I	W	A	N
Y	I	A	F	L	R	Z	E	H	Y	F	X	J	C	S	X	H	C	C	D
S	N	I	I	A	M	A	N	O	I	S	E	A	T	O	U	W	X	Y	E
J	G	N	U	N	E	X	T	V	L	C	Y	R	I	F	S	W	Q	Y	R
E	A	I	R	G	N	T	K	X	N	T	I	G	O	S	Z	E	D	C	S
A	B	N	U	U	T	Z	Z	E	E	Q	E	O	N	P	O	H	K	H	T
L	U	G	P	A	S	O	D	I	Y	T	K	N	L	E	K	H	X	E	A
C	A	J	K	G	D	I	X	F	I	Y	N	N	O	E	C	G	A	C	N
O	L	V	B	E	F	N	A	N	R	S	Q	Q	O	C	M	Z	Y	K	D
H	Y	P	H	N	A	D	D	Y	E	N	F	S	P	H	A	X	O	I	I
O	Y	K	O	H	B	A	G	G	R	E	S	S	I	O	N	K	U	N	N
L	W	C	J	C	G	H	I	O	H	K	Z	J	M	T	D	W	D	G	G
F	V	R	D	J	T	I	N	T	E	R	P	R	E	T	E	R	N	G	M

impairments   advocacy   training   induction loop   confidence   jargon   noise
aggression   alcohol   understanding   repeating   health   language   anxiety
interpreter   signing   checking   dialects   figures of speech

Demonstrate strategies to clarify misunderstandings

The following activity helps you to think about ways to resolve communication difficulties and misunderstandings. These may occur with individuals in your care or with colleagues.

ACTIVITY

Complete the gaps in the following sentences using the words listed below.

figures of speech   aggression   interpreter   alcohol   induction loop   checking   training   anxiety   dialects

❀ It could be easier for someone to hear if they use an _____ _____.

❀ Drinking _____ can affect the way you think and speak.

❀ The ability and awareness of staff is enhanced by the correct _____.

❀ The English language is difficult when people use _____ _____ _____ instead of the correct word.

❀ A good knowledge of your subject gives you _____ to use it.

❀ Ignoring someone, or not listening properly, could lead to possible _____ or threats.

❀ In some circumstances, it may be beneficial to employ an _____ when talking to a person whose first language is not English.

❀ Regional _____ may lead to misunderstandings.

❀ If you are not completely sure of what is required, _____ before starting is advisable.

❀ Not fully understanding what is being said or asked can lead to a state of _____.

Managing a meeting

Consider your first day at work at a health and social care setting. You may know very little about the workings of the unit and you have no idea what would be on an agenda or what would need to be discussed in a meeting. As you learn about your duties, it will become clear to you what issues are important and need to be discussed. Observe your manager carrying out his or her duties and imagine that one day you, too, may have to think more deeply about the issues featured in the next activity. This may be a good start for you to test your knowledge.

ACTIVITY

Mark has been promoted in the residential home for people with learning difficulties where he works.

He has noticed that certain jobs could be done differently to improve the home and benefit the residents; he has also observed that some of the staff are quite lazy. He calls a meeting but isn't sure how to deal with the issues and manage a large team. Items on the meeting's agenda are 'Health and safety', 'Equality, diversity and inclusion', 'Safeguarding issues' and 'Training and development needs'. Place the numbers of his jumbled thoughts under the correct heading so that the meeting runs smoothly. Be aware that some items may need to go under more than one heading.

1. The night staff need to be disciplined; they are too noisy and there have been complaints.

2. The younger residents are bored and too restricted.

3. Some older residents are displaying negative emotions.

4. The cleaner spotted a mouse; hygiene is poor.

5. Risk assessments are not documented properly.

6. Some staff have no idea about data protection.

7. Some staff have low morale.

8. There is little provision for religious practices.

What should Mark do?

Health and safety

Equality, diversity and inclusion

Safeguarding issues

Training and development needs

Negotiation, flexibility and reporting

There are times in the health and social care sector when you will need to be flexible in order to ensure the best care for that individual. People have rights and choices under a variety of legislation, especially the Care Standards Act (2000), the Mental Capacity Act (2005) and the Human Rights Act (1998). The Care Quality Commission (CQC) regulates practice and ensures compliance with the National Occupational Standards (NOS).

ACTIVITY

1. Research the requirements under each Act, the role of the CQC and the NOS for health and social care. One requirement is that people are to be encouraged to self-medicate where possible.

2. Read the following scenario and decide on the best approach that gives flexibility, scope to negotiate and ensures you are not in breach of any legislation or codes of practice.

Mr Needham

Mr Needham is a registered drug user and attends a needle exchange. He lives alone but efforts are being made by Social Services to help rehabilitate him so that he will no longer be dependent on the drugs. He has now been prescribed oral medication, a controlled drug called temazepam. You are his visiting support worker and he assures you he will remember to take it. He doesn't want you to give it to him every time he needs it.

3. What do you say to him? The table shows some of the things you could say. Tick the most appropriate response, with a short comment in the right-hand column explaining your views about each possible response.

Response	Your views on the response
I am sorry, Mr Needham, it is my right to visit you and make sure you take this medication.	
You know you have not got much willpower and have a poor memory. Better that I see to it.	
There are so many records to complete that it would make life easier if I came every day.	
It is not my decision, it's the law. However, if you get better I won't need to come.	
You have the right so you can take it yourself.	
I am listening to you but I must conduct a risk assessment to ensure you are capable. This will need to be looked at again periodically.	

How to access extra support and services to enable effective communication

Different people in your care will have different needs. It is important to remember that to help someone effectively you need to contact people with expertise in that area.

Support agencies, equipment and resources

ACTIVITY

Use an internet search engine to find out about agencies that can provide extra support and services to enable effective communication and identify what they provide. In the second column, write the name of one or more agencies that support the condition listed. In the third column, identify a piece of equipment or resource to help that person communicate effectively. An example has been done for you.

Condition	Supporting agencies	Resource or equipment
Impaired speech.	Connect and Afasic	Signing material/pictorial aids/software. Counselling via Skype.
Hearing impaired.		
Sight impaired.		
Learning impaired.		

Apply principles and practices relating to confidentiality

Confidentiality is an important aspect of working with individuals in health and social care. Regulatory bodies provide guidance on what confidentiality means in practice and the limits and boundaries to confidentiality. Look at the following websites to find out more about this guidance.

* www.cqc.org.uk
* www.cafcass.gov.uk
* www.dh.gov.uk

key term

Confidentiality: ensuring that information is accessible only to those authorised to have access.

Ways to maintain confidentiality in day-to-day communication

When you meet a person in a care setting for the first time you will need to ask lots of questions about their medical history and personal details. You must tell them that information is only disclosed on a 'need-to-know' basis and that all records are secured safely. Confidentiality relates to the communication of all types of information, whether it is spoken, written or electronic.

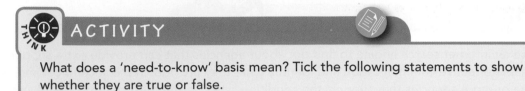

ACTIVITY

What does a 'need-to-know' basis mean? Tick the following statements to show whether they are true or false.

TRUE/FALSE

- A GP has a right to share information with another expert.
- A carer has full rights to an individual's health records.
- An individual has a right to see their own health records.
- A carer must pass on to the next of kin details of addresses and contact number of care services.

Your questions answered...

What does 'information gathered on a need-to know-basis' mean?

This refers to details that may be needed if there is an accident at work or that would be of interest to statutory bodies, health agencies or inspectorates, such as CVs and evidence of appropriate qualifications. Examples of details include: families' addresses and contact numbers, known allergies and medical conditions that are important for continuity of care.

All health and social care organisations will have guidance on the correct procedures for managing information and maintaining confidentiality in order to comply with legislation. The Data Protection Act 1998 relates to the gathering, handling and storing of information, the Human Rights Act Article 8 relates to an individual's right to privacy and the Freedom of Information Act 2000 covers access to information which doesn't include personal details and which is not included in the Data Protection Act.

Other legislation that will have influenced organisational policies and procedures includes the Mental Capacity Act 2005, which ensures procedures are in place to support individuals who lack the capacity to make a decision and the Computer Misuse Act 1990, which secures computer programs and data through authorisation protocols and makes unauthorised access or alteration a criminal offence.

The next activity will test your knowledge and awareness of what is sensitive information and whether you need to disclose some personal information to colleagues. Not disclosing it is usually done to protect that person's health and welfare.

ACTIVITY

Look at the information below and decide whether you think it might be sensitive information. Explain your decision briefly in the last column.

Information given to you	Sensitive information? Yes/No	Why?
I am HIV-positive.		
My sister takes drugs.		
I live in an apartment.		
My contact telephone numbers are …		
I can't tell you how I got my bruises; it's not your business.		
Don't let my husband in to see me, please.		

Potential tensions between maintaining an individual's confidentiality and disclosing concerns

There may be times during your work when you come across something you think is wrong. Remember, it is your statutory duty to report concerns of a sensitive nature to your line manager and to maintain any confidential records securely. It is important for you to know the procedure for handling disclosed information. You will need to consider the following.

- The level of urgency in passing on information. For example, is there a level of danger involved?
- The appropriate person to speak to. For example, this may be your manager or someone from an outside agency, such as CQC.
- How to pass the information on. For example, would it be best as a verbal or written report?

Remember to maintain confidentiality when passing on information that has been disclosed to you, as this is likely to be on a 'need-to-know' basis.

ACTIVITY

Carry out some research using the 'Essential Standards of Quality and Safety' PDF on the CQC website (www.cqc.org.uk/standards) and other websites, to find two reasons when you should disclose information given to you and not hold this as confidential.

-
-

Undesirable practices and the procedures for reporting concerns

Read the case study below and answer the questions that follow it. It may be useful to discuss your answers with your colleagues.

Ushmita

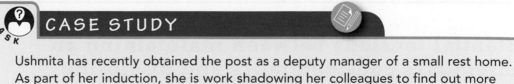

CASE STUDY

Ushmita has recently obtained the post as a deputy manager of a small rest home. As part of her induction, she is work shadowing her colleagues to find out more about the procedures and policies of the setting. However, she quickly notices that there are undesirable practices here. She observes the following.

- Care plans are not up-to-date and there are no person-centred risk assessments.

✿ Some residents are not offered a mid-morning or mid-afternoon drink because they do not come to the lounge.

✿ There are no infection control policies and there is no guidance for the staff.

✿ There has been no training on safeguarding for many years.

✿ There is a shortage of staff on duty at night and no risk assessment has been carried out to cover this.

✿ A couple of carers are not following person-centred approaches and are quite abrupt in their manner with certain vulnerable residents.

✿ There does not appear to be a policy on whistle-blowing or a complaints policy.

1. What outcomes of the 'Essential standards of quality and safety' are involved?

2. What are a complaints procedure and a policy on whistle-blowing?

3. What should Ushmita do?

Ushmita makes some observations

4. What can be done to reduce the risk of abuse or harm addressing all the above observations?

5. How can a setting ensure that all staff are aware of safeguarding policies, standards and procedures?

ARE YOU READY FOR ASSESSMENT?

☑ **Do you know the following:**

- [ ] **1.** The reasons why people communicate?

- [ ] **2.** How communication affects working relationships?

- [ ] **3.** The factors that promote effective communication?

- [ ] **4.** How individuals from different backgrounds use or interpret communication differently?

- [ ] **5.** How to identify barriers to effective communication?

- [ ] **6.** How to access extra support or services to ensure individuals can communicate more effectively?

- [ ] **7.** The meaning of confidentiality?

- [ ] **8.** The potential tensions between an individual's confidentiality and disclosing concerns?

☑ **Can you do the following:**

- [ ] **1.** Establish an individual's language needs, wishes and preferences?

- [ ] **2.** Use a range of communication methods and styles to meet individual needs, wishes and preferences?

- [ ] **3.** Respond to an individual's reactions when communicating?

- [ ] **4.** Demonstrate ways to overcome barriers to communication?

- [ ] **5.** Use different strategies to clarify misunderstandings?

- [ ] **6.** Maintain confidentiality of information through your daily work activities?

UNIT SHC 32

Engage in personal development in health and social care settings

This unit will help you to be more aware of yourself, to look at your achievements and qualifications, the role and responsibilities expected of you in certain jobs within the sector, and how you can make plans to improve your skills to progress in your career. It is important for you to focus on where you want to be in the future and draw up plans that will help you to achieve that goal.

Everyone needs to keep up to date in their jobs in order to meet the requirements of new laws and to improve the service for those they care for. It also benefits you by developing your professionalism, your self-esteem and your chances of promotion.

You will need to be able to:
* understand what is required for competence in your own work role
* reflect on practice
* evaluate your performance
* agree a personal development plan
* use learning opportunities and reflective practice to contribute to personal development.

What is required for competence in your own work role?

Describe the duties and responsibilities of your own work role

When you apply for a job, it is assumed that you have read the requirements of the role so that you know what you are expected to do.

A job description describes the job – the main areas of responsibility and the tasks that need to be undertaken. A specification (often called a person specification or job specification) describes the ideal candidate for doing the job. It will list the skills, qualifications and experience that are required.

Some person specifications will highlight the essential requirements (what you must know) and the desirable requirements (things you may not know, but for which training will be given).

ACTIVITY

Read the two person specifications and, for each requirement, tick the appropriate column to indicate whether, in your opinion, they are essential or desirable requirements for the role.

Position: Senior Care Worker in a residential and nursing home for older people

Role description	Essential requirements	Desirable requirements
Be able to communicate effectively using verbal, non-verbal and written methods.		
Work within the legal frameworks and the National Occupational Standards (NOS) for the sector.		
Follow the policies and procedures of the organisation.		
Be able to liaise with the medical team.		
Manage unit duties and rotas of care assistants.		
Administer medications and oxygen when necessary.		
Participate in staff meetings.		
Maintain care plans using a holistic focus.		
Be qualified to Level 3 standard.		

Position: Community Support Worker

Role description	Essential requirements	Desirable requirements
Be able to relate well to people and their families in a community setting.		

Role description	Essential requirements	Desirable requirements
Be able to work autonomously and use initiative while working within policy guidelines.		
Contribute to the organisation's safeguarding ethos by following procedures.		
Contribute to building positive relationships with people and families.		
Be able to write reports in accordance with policy and maintain care plans.		
Work within established codes of practice.		
Be qualified to Level 4 in the health and social care sector (or be working towards it).		
Monitor and advise people and families on all health and safety matters.		
Occasionally give presentations to the local authority.		

Expectations about your own work role as expressed in relevant standards

Guidance is provided for you in various formats and it is useful to keep revisiting these as an individual and a group (in team meetings) so you can all agree whether you are complying with requirements for good practice. These include **codes of practice** and the **National Minimum Standards**. Most organisations work in compliance with a set code of professional practice behaviours. Examples may relate to dress, confidentiality, duty of care and adhering to the **National Occupational Standards** (NOS).

Standards are also set out in two pieces of legislation: the Health and Social Care Act 2008 (Regulated Activities) Regulations 2010 and the Care Quality Commission (Registration) Regulations 2009. There is a set of 16 **Essential Standards of Quality and Safety**, each with an outcome that will be used to measure the quality and safety standards that care providers have in place. You will need to research these on the internet.

ACTIVITY

If you do not have a copy of the GSCC Codes of Practice for Social Care Workers, you can find it at www.gscc.org.uk/page/91/Get+copies+of+our+codes.html. You can locate the CQC Essential Standards of Quality and Safety from www.cqc.org.uk/standards. Using both documents complete the following activity.

Complete the two tables that follow by identifying four more standards from each set of standards that describe what a competent worker is expected to do. The first one in each table has been done for you.

According to the GSCC Codes of Practice for Social Care Workers, a competent worker is one who:

Maintains clear and accurate records as required by procedures established for their work (GSCC Code of Practice 6.2).

According to the CQC Essential Standards of Quality and Safety, a competent worker is one who:

Understands the signs of abuse and can raise this with the right person when those signs are noticed (CQC Essential Standards Outcome 7A).

Standards

ACTIVITY

Identify the key words in the wordsearch. These words will appear within the text of the National Occupational Standards or National Minimum Standards. They are words that you will see when considering your personal development and reflecting on practice.

R	Y	Y	S	B	H	M	O	T	I	V	A	T	I	O	N	Y	H	E	A
E	S	S	L	V	N	R	E	V	I	E	W	C	P	W	T	C	M	K	R
S	B	A	S	F	P	R	O	F	E	S	S	I	O	N	A	L	I	S	M
O	C	F	V	D	Z	U	R	I	A	L	J	V	H	C	E	H	M	H	D
L	Q	E	X	M	E	V	D	T	C	Q	V	S	F	L	V	H	S	E	R
V	N	G	P	Q	C	X	R	P	C	Y	E	Y	O	R	Y	E	A	A	E
E	V	U	M	B	G	D	C	Q	O	R	Q	R	G	Y	I	A	Z	L	P
S	T	A	N	D	A	R	D	S	U	W	I	T	E	R	V	F	B	T	O
H	C	R	E	D	A	T	X	D	N	I	H	E	E	H	O	W	H	H	R
V	Y	D	W	F	T	T	E	M	T	H	Z	U	W	D	X	Y	C	A	T
A	D	I	D	Y	L	C	O	O	A	H	Q	K	A	M	B	M	G	N	I
N	W	N	O	B	O	C	D	V	B	K	S	J	T	O	V	P	Y	D	N
A	K	G	D	R	G	E	H	Z	I	S	E	L	A	N	K	P	A	S	G
L	J	G	P	I	Q	S	O	Y	L	X	A	R	P	I	F	F	I	A	L
Y	U	R	E	S	P	O	N	S	I	B	I	L	I	T	I	E	S	F	T
S	Q	J	E	M	Y	M	Q	V	T	G	L	J	F	O	C	I	J	E	G
I	R	S	M	W	J	M	L	K	Y	T	V	L	T	R	Y	U	N	T	R
S	C	L	R	E	F	L	E	C	T	I	O	N	Z	G	J	J	I	Y	W
E	C	T	E	S	T	I	D	E	A	S	B	Z	X	Z	V	C	T	L	T
Y	G	V	D	K	U	O	I	M	D	W	F	R	I	A	S	S	E	S	S

safeguarding   reflection   log   health and safety   assess   motivation   queries
test ideas   monitor   resolve   role   accountability   review   analysis   reporting
professionalism   procedures   standards   responsibilities

Self-development

ACTIVITY

Across

1. A goal (6)
5. An observable act (11)
7. Your specific duties are highlighted in this document. The first word is 'Job' (11)
8. A different view can be referred to as this (11)
9. To make judgements (8)
12. Abiding by rules (12)
13. When should patient care always come? (5)
14. You might do this to increase knowledge and skills (8)
16. You need this to make progress (10)

Down

2. Thinking about the way we do things is commonly viewed as this (10)
3. To criticise oneself may be looked at in this way in order to make improvements (10)
4. Understanding the principles of protection of human rights is now given this term (12)
6. Health and social care workers are all given national guidelines referred to as what? (9)
7. To show how you do something (11)
10. Inspectors will look at this to judge standards (8)
11. A signed document to indicate agreement and compliance to policies and procedures (8)
15. Thinking of something new or different (4)

Be able to reflect on practice

The importance of reflective practice in continuously improving the quality of service

Working with people requires you to be able to adapt your approach to meet their individual needs and expectations. Reflecting on your practice enables you to not only evaluate your work but to learn more about which approaches work and why. This enables you to develop the range of responses and strategies you can use to work effectively with people.

Reflective practice helps you to analyse and evaluate key interactions or specific situations so that you can be fully aware of what you did. This increases your self-awareness: the thoughts and feelings that affected your responses. It helps you to look at the interaction or situation from a different perspective. This then helps you to challenge assumptions, identify patterns of behaviour, test out other approaches, make links between theory and practice and recognise areas for future development.

Reflection is an important tool in helping you to learn and develop your practice. Reflection is a continuous process. As you can see from the diagram below, there is always more to learn.

Various models have been devised and proposed to show how people learn. People use different methods. Some may watch an activity before doing it, some may go straight into it using trial and error, others may read and think about it, and others may try it out after a brief problem-solving session. Much of the learning in the health and social care sector is done by watching, listening, practising and, particularly, **reflective practice**.

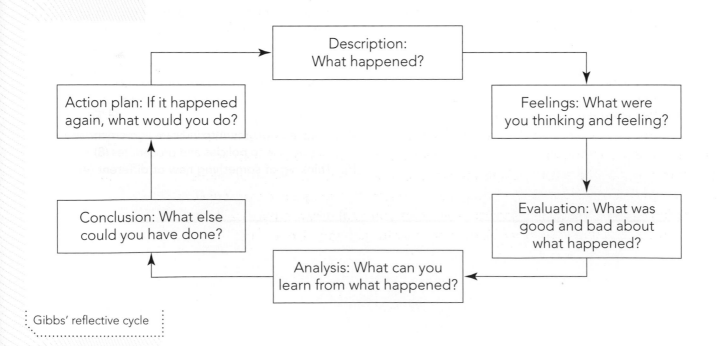

Gibbs' reflective cycle

You may find it useful to research David Kolb's experiential learning cycle and Peter Honey and Alan Mumford's model (adapted from the Kolb model).

These different styles of learning are often termed VAK which stands for **visual, auditory and kinaesthetic**. A mix of styles can sometimes be better than one, but for certain people learning using one style may keep them motivated.

Learning opportunities: demonstrate the ability to reflect on practice

ACTIVITY

Imagine that you have secured the job of the Senior Care Worker from the activity on page 25, but you are required to do some tasks that you have not performed before. Look at the tasks in the boxes on the left and draw a line to match the most appropriate **initial** learning opportunity given in the right-hand boxes

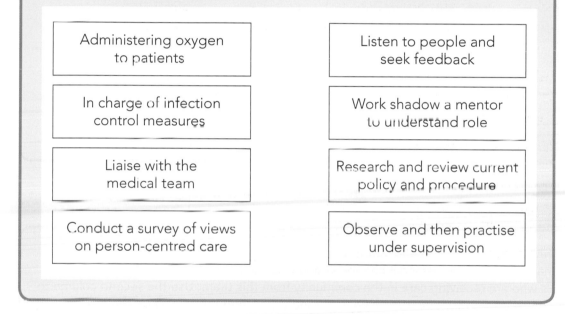

Administering oxygen to patients	Listen to people and seek feedback
In charge of infection control measures	Work shadow a mentor to understand role
Liaise with the medical team	Research and review current policy and procedure
Conduct a survey of views on person-centred care	Observe and then practise under supervision

How do your own values, beliefs and experiences affect working practice?

You will work with a range of different colleagues throughout your career and also with a range of individuals who will be in your care. Not everyone is the same, and they may not share your beliefs and standards. Many factors influence values and beliefs. These include family background, cultural and religious background, education (such as the type of school experience you had), environment (such as your home and where you grew up), economic status and moral influences.

ACTIVITY

Think about your own life experience and identify three main influences on your values and beliefs, and the reasons why you think they had the greatest influence.

The three main influences on my values and beliefs are:

1.

Reason:

2.

Reason:

3.

Reason:

ACTIVITY

1. Imagine you work with a team of carers, who you get to know quite well over a short space of time. Listed below are 'snapshots' of their personal prejudices and dislikes. Read about the carers and then the list of individuals who are receiving care in the community from this team. Use the second column to briefly explain how these values may affect the care of the individual, and the effects on the carer.

   ✿ Miriam hates smoking and feels sick when around any smell of tobacco.
   ✿ Charlie has difficulties caring for obese people. All his life he has been told he is fat because he is lazy.
   ✿ Carmen becomes very angry when people use bad language. She also dislikes people who get drunk and have 'no purpose' in life.

The individual in the community	Explain the possible effect of the care values on the experience of both the carer and the individual
Miriam visits Mrs Hall, who is a heavy smoker.	

The individual in the community	Explain the possible effect of the care values on the experience of both the carer and the individual
Charlie visits Tom, who is significantly overweight and blames it on long-term treatment with steroids.	
Carmen visits Lola, a recovering alcoholic and drug abuser who swears constantly.	

2. Summarise your personal 'snapshot' of one of your dislikes or beliefs. Explain how you may need to balance your views when caring for individuals.

A personal dislike or belief	Explain how this may affect your work and the care experience of others

3. In the first column, list what other values and beliefs may affect care experiences. Use the second column to summarise what actions can support carers whose beliefs and prejudices may affect care experiences.

List other values and beliefs that may affect the care experience	Summarise the actions that can support carers whose beliefs and prejudices may affect work

Giving feedback to others

ACTIVITY

Giving feedback is an important part of working with people as it helps them to know what they are doing well and what, if anything, needs to change. When feedback is given in a constructive way it will encourage and motivate people to do their best and enjoy their job. Constructive feedback needs to be SMARTER.

Specific – clear, precise and detailed (NOS can be used to keep comments specific and objective).

Measurable – you are able to identify the change.

Accurate – true and about the person and the situation.

Reliable – it is backed by objective evidence not personal opinion.

Timely – given to the person at the appropriate time and, if needed, timescales for achievement are agreed.

Educational – if focused on helping the person to learn.

Respectful – recognises the individual by respecting their privacy and individual needs.

Observe a colleague working with a service user and then think about how you could give them constructive feedback to encourage and motivate them, using SMARTER as a guide.

Negative feedback

Sometimes managers or colleagues may not feel at all positive about a certain situation or issue. This could be because of things that have happened or have been said to them in the past, or because they have had bad experiences of caring for disadvantaged groups. They may also have negative perceptions and there may be conflicts in implementing any changes. These colleagues may not want to contribute to any suggested improvements.

Affecting working practice

ACTIVITY

Think about the feedback you have given for the previous activity or about feedback that may have been given to you. The table below lists some actions you could take as a result of this feedback. Circle the action(s) that you would carry out to ensure that your values, beliefs and experiences do not affect your working practice. Finally, comment on the effect that each action would have on colleagues and service users.

Actions	Comments
Ignore the feedback for now and move on.	
Challenge the feedback, explaining you've done your best.	
Look at the positive feedback first and address the negative aspects last.	
Resign.	
Acknowledge all the feedback, reflect and act upon it.	
Analyse the feedback in detail and find explanations for it.	
Share your frustration with other colleagues or service users.	

Evaluate your performance

Evaluate your own knowledge, performance and understanding

The health and social care sector needs to ensure their workers are up to date with changes of policy and standards. You will have regular supervision periods with your line manager to identify any gaps in your knowledge and to ensure you are confident in carrying out your duties. Your annual appraisal will also identify how you are progressing and maintaining your professionalism in accordance with the standards.

Matching the standards

 ACTIVITY

Read the outcome summaries extracted from the Essential Standards of Quality and Safety (Health and Social Care Act 2008, Regulated Activities) Regulations 2010 and the Care Quality Commission (Registration) Regulations 2009.

Summarise duties you carry out that will show evidence that you meet this outcome. An example has been done for you.

Regulation (outcome)	Summary of outcome	How I evidence this in my practice (use a particular task)
9(4) Care and welfare.	People experience safe, appropriate care and treatments, supporting needs and rights.	Personal care: I check that all physical needs are met, that the person has what he or she needs for a bath, including mobility aids. I check the cleanliness of the bathroom before starting to run the bath and ensure that towels and face cloths are clean. I check that clean clothes are ready to put on after the bath. I check whether the person can manage with me alone or if I need to ask for someone to help me.
10(16) Assessing and monitoring quality of provision.	The management of risk assessments ensure people benefit from safe quality care.	
12(8) Cleanliness and infection control.	People experience a clean environment protected from acquiring infections.	
21(12) Requirements relating to workers.	People are safe; health and welfare needs are met by staff who possess the correct qualifications and skills.	
23 (14) Supporting workers.	People are kept safe; health and welfare needs are met because staff are competent to carry out duties, are properly trained, supervised and appraised.	

ACTIVITY

Complete the gaps in the following passage using the words listed below. The passage indicates changes made to service delivery in a residential home for people with mental health issues.

health   safety   risk   food   safeguarding   risk assessment
person-centred   infection control   first aid

* Great Hall has increased the number of employees who now hold a current _____ _____ qualification. We have reviewed our policy in the event of a cardiac arrest.

* Eight employees have gained a _____ safety, qualification and they have special responsibility for amending the care plans in terms of allergies and conditions affecting diet.

* All 24 employees have attended _____ training, which included the Mental Capacity Act and its implications on practice.

* The following week they attended a 'Recognition of Equality and Diversity' workshop. This included ways of involving all residents in various _____-_____ activities and this helped to update our knowledge and awareness of spotting potential hazards for a _____ _____ course.

* Four of the 24 employees are now representatives having completed a _____ and _____ course. They can be consulted on all aspects of _____ _____, having conducted a review of the high _____ ____ areas that include toilets, kitchens and clinical areas.

The use of feedback to evaluate own performance and improve developments

Feedback can be given using forms, such as those from a regulatory body like the CQC (which is about the provision as a whole setting) or from your manager during supervision or at appraisal times. You can make better use of the supervision and appraisal opportunities if you prepare well beforehand. Use the supervision agenda to identify areas of your practice where you would like feedback. Don't wait to receive feedback on those areas of practice your supervisor has identified, as these may be different to the areas which you are concerned about or require reassurance. Supervision and appraisal are both two-way processes, but only if you take an active part in them.

Thorough preparation will help you achieve this and help you become more confident and competent in your practice. Your employer should have supervision and appraisal policies and guidance on how to make the best use of both processes. Feedback can also be informal, such as when someone observes you or accompanies you on a task. Individuals may also comment on your performance, informing you of what works and what doesn't.

ACTIVITY

Read the scenario below and write a report to indicate how you would make improvements (using a positive report-writing style), as if you were the manager of this residential and care home. You have been given some key terms and issues to help you, but be be aware that some are not relevant! Use the sub-headings given as guidance and include the relevant issues as you think is best. Include some ideas of your own.

Scenario

Montgomery House Nursing and Residential Care Home has actions from the recent inspection by the CQC. They include insufficient attention to person-centred care and planning, and also too many minor errors when staff are administering medication. It was noted that residents are bored and there was an impression of regimentation in seating arrangements.

Issues to consider

- ✿ Seek advice from the pharmacist.
- ✿ Review the care plans in terms of meeting NOS.
- ✿ Research the Handling of Medicines in Social Work 2007.
- ✿ Research person-centred care practice.
- ✿ Research the Food Standards Agency.
- ✿ Research the Disability and Discrimination Act.
- ✿ Research the Mental Capacity Act Deprivation of Liberty Safeguards.
- ✿ Research activities for older people in residential care to do.
- ✿ Develop a policy and procedure for trainees when administering medications.
- ✿ Research training opportunities and funding for training for Understanding the Safe Handling of Medicines (QCF).
- ✿ Research the cost of new seats for the living area.
- ✿ Monitor the recording of the MAR sheets.

Your sub-headings

Action 1: Insufficient attention to person-centred care and planning

I would address this by

Action 2: Too many minor errors when staff are administering medication

I would address this by

Action 3: Residents appear bored

I would address this by

Action 4: Seating arrangements are regimented

I would address this by

Be able to agree a personal development plan

When you start work in the sector, your manager will introduce you to the **Common Induction Standards**.

As you progress in the sector, you may be asked to do certain jobs that you have not done before. Never agree to do a task unless you have been shown how to do it properly and understand the issues related to that task.

Always ask for help when you are unsure of anything. You should make sure you fully understand how to perform a task and receive help and support to do every task so you can perform it competently on your own. Your personal development plan (PDP) is the means by which you can record your competence at the time of writing it; identify the areas for development; show how you plan to meet those development needs; record how you will evaluate and review your progress and give timescales for doing this. It is an important document that you need to refer to regularly, such as at supervision meetings, so that you can check you are progressing as planned and adapt your plans if they are not working. Make sure your learning outcomes are SMARTER: Specific, Measurable, Accurate, Realistic, Timely, Educational and Respectful.

key term

Common Induction Standards: a set of eight standards (mapped across the diploma) that form the induction process into the care sector.

Sources of support for planning and reviewing own development

There are many options to help you to review and develop professionally but a close and experienced source is your line manager. At the beginning of this unit you looked at different learning methods, so think about how you learn best. For example, you might learn effectively from reading about issues and then applying this new knowledge in the workplace. It might also help to speak to other health professionals, perhaps those who visit the setting where you work (for example a physiotherapist or occupational therapist) or who work close by, such as the pharmacist.

ACTIVITY

Complete the table below by listing the possible sources of support to help you to develop your knowledge, understanding and care practice. Think about the people who could support you, as well as other types of resource. For each one, identify how these sources would support your own development. An example has been done for you.

Source of support	How this would support your development
Line manager.	Feedback on practice, information on policies and procedures.

Work with others to review and prioritise own learning needs, professional interests and development opportunities

ACTIVITY

Look at the eight Common Induction Standards in the left-hand column. In the second column, indicate at least one aspect of each standard that you need to show evidence of applying in the workplace. In the last column, indicate what you would like to know or practise. This should then be discussed in your next appraisal or supervision session. Remember that you are entitled to be given regular opportunities to discuss your personal development.

Common Induction standards	An example from my practice to show as evidence	What I need to ask my manager
Role of the health and social care worker.		
Personal development.		
Communicate effectively.		
Equality and diversity issues.		
Principles for implementing duty of care.		
Principles for safeguarding.		
Person-centred support.		
Health and safety in adult social care.		

How to work with others to agree a personal development plan

ACTIVITY

The following table shows some competences that are required within the health and social care sector, you may wish to think of some of your own. Check your knowledge for each one. Columns two to four indicate how competent you are to carry out each duty or responsibility. The fourth column indicates where you need training or practice. Based on your evaluation, you can set yourself a task to increase your knowledge and application of skills. Target dates for achieving the skill may be included here. You may wish to copy the table onto a separate piece of paper.

Skill or knowledge	I am proficient in this and I have a good understanding. Add last date of training or update.	I need support in this area. Add any research and work shadowing opportunities or personnel who can support you.	Indicate external training needs and dates. Add date when arranged.
Administering oral medications and **subcutaneous injections**.			
Ordering medications.			
Recording risk assessments.			
Using a hoist.			
Barrier nursing an infectious patient.			
Performing **CPR**.			
Carrying out interviews to amend care plans.			
Applying safeguarding procedures of the setting.			

Use learning opportunities and reflective practice for your personal development

How learning activities have affected practice and led to improved ways of working

You will have noted that knowledge is acquired and applied in practice. That practice is constantly evaluated in terms of its quality and value for users of care services. If you don't think a method of working is helping people, then measures should be taken to change the procedures so that it does. One example of this in recent years is the shift towards person-centred care instead of being 'task orientated'. The benefits to health and well-being are much greater with person-centred care.

You need to think of ways to record your learning and thoughts about practice. The following activity is one way of recording learning opportunities and the application of learning into practice.

Record progress in relation to personal development

ACTIVITY

You can record your progress by maintaining your CV and updating it when you achieve a qualification, have work shadowed someone or attended an event or conference. This should enable you to make progress that improves your professionalism and the quality of care given to others.

Look at examples of CVs on the internet and choose a layout that suits you. Do not put in too much information but be concise about what you have achieved, when you achieved it, how you achieved it (accreditation) and what benefits it gave you in practice. You will need your educational history, employment history and (if you wish) a little about your interests and personal beliefs (sometimes referred to as your 'ethos'). Never use the words 'I feel'; instead, use strong words such as 'I do' or 'I think'.

You could also ask a friend, colleague or manager to read your CV and provide you with any feedback.

Assessor tip

When you have almost completed your diploma, have a reflective discussion with your assessor as this will really help you to recognise and appreciate how far you have progressed, as well as providing good portfolio evidence.

Reflecting on learning opportunities

ACTIVITY

Imagine you have now completed the training opportunities in the left-hand column. Describe what you need to do now to ensure you progress with competence and confidence.

Learning opportunity	What I need to do now to ensure I am safe to practise
Administering oral medications and subcutaneous injections: I have now given oral medications with a senior worker and have been shown once how to do a subcutaneous injection.	
Ordering and disposing of medications: I have been shown the order book and the disposal record book for the pharmacist but have not completed the details.	
Recording risk assessments: I have been shown how to risk assess for lifting a person using one hoist but not the other two. I have not been shown a general health and safety check.	
Person-centred care planning: I have completed training and know how to gather history notes but have not yet conducted an interview with an individual.	

Your questions answered...

Why should I monitor and review my knowledge and skills?

Legislation develops according to what has happened within the sector; it keeps changing in order to improve ways of working. The requirements for practice are passed down to various organisations and incorporated into their policies and procedures. If you do not keep up to date you could make a serious mistake that is a breach of your contract and perhaps break the law.

key term

Tangible evidence: evidence that can be seen, measured or examined.

Angelina

Angelina had worked for four years as a community care worker and a health care assistant in a hospital. She felt she had gathered enough knowledge and skills to train others. She was asked to mentor new recruits and enjoyed this so decided to begin teaching and work shadowed a lecturer. However, she knew she would need a higher qualification.

As Angelina was married and had young children, she was apprehensive about the time and commitment that studying would take and how this might impact her home life. She discussed her concerns with her husband, who agreed to help more with the children, and with a college tutor during an interview.

Angelina now has time to study

She was surprised at how flexible the arrangements and timetable could be. She was also pleased that some of the tasks related to her job role. She discussed her plans with her current manager, who was equally helpful with changing shifts to help her study. This gave her time with her family as well as time to study, and she practised more teaching of staff in her current role.

She was told that the best way to achieve her qualification was to keep to targets and try not to let submission dates slip. In the end, she had **tangible evidence** of her achievements.

1. What persuaded Angelina to take another career pathway?

2. What were her concerns?

3. How did people help her?

4. Apart from engaging in study, what other activities helped her progression?

5. What was one important piece of advice?

6. Why is it important for people to have a goal in terms of their career?

7. What do you think is tangible evidence of Angelina's achievements?

ARE YOU READY FOR ASSESSMENT?

☑ **Do you know the following:**

☐ 1. The main duties and responsibilities of your job role?

☐ 2. The standards that help you understand what is expected of you in your job role?

☐ 3. The importance of reflective practice as a way to improve the quality of your work?

☐ 4. How your values, attitudes, belief systems and experiences have affected your work practice?

☐ 5. Identify sources of support to develop your knowledge, understanding and skills?

☑ **Can you do the following:**

☐ 1. Reflect on your work practice?

☐ 2. Evaluate your knowledge, performance and understanding against relevant standards?

☐ 3. Use feedback to evaluate your performance and inform your development?

☐ 4. Work with others to review and prioritise your learning needs, professional interests and development opportunities?

☐ 5. Work with others to develop and agree your personal development plan?

☐ 6. Evaluate how learning opportunities and reflection have affected and improved your work practice?

☐ 7. Show how reflective practice has led to improved ways of working?

☐ 8. Show how to record progress in relation to personal development?

UNIT SHC 33

Promote equality and inclusion in health and social care settings

This unit provides you with the knowledge to give you a better understanding of diversity, equality and inclusion. This knowledge and awareness will help you to create a care environment that promotes equality, supports diversity and avoids the potentially harmful effects of discrimination.

You will need to be able to:

❁ understand the importance of diversity, equality and inclusion

❁ work in an inclusive way

❁ promote diversity, equality and inclusion.

The importance of diversity, equality and inclusion

Diversity

We are all very different as people in terms of where we were born, where we live and how we live, but there are many things about humans that are universal: in particular, we all have a similar range of emotions. Other people's behaviours and beliefs may be different, but we all deserve respect and the right to be accepted for who we are. It is natural to make judgements about people we meet, but it is harder for us to be non-judgemental by accepting **diversity** and other people's choices and preferences without prejudice.

It is too easy to **stereotype** people, that is, to make assumptions based on what people are usually thought of being like and what we are familiar with.

<aside>
key terms

Diversity: differences between individuals and groups, for example, culture, race, gender, religion, age, abilities and disabilities, sexual orientation and social class.

Stereotype: perceiving people as a certain type, according to how they dress or behave.
</aside>

ACTIVITY

Read the following descriptions of people who you might find in any community.

Neil is 42, lives in a very large house and wears suits when he goes out.

Anita is 34 and sits on the balcony of her small fourth-floor rented flat, reading, for most of the day.

Talek goes to work on his bicycle, wears trainers and a peaked cap.

Crawford likes to wear bright colours and listen to loud music.

Christine is 80, is a wheelchair user and is often seen tending a raised garden.

Read the following occupations and estimate how people may perceive the characters on page 49, by matching a job to a stereotypical person image below. Give your reasons.

Who is the doctor?

Who is unemployed?

Who is studying for a degree?

Who is the professional sports person?

Who is the lawyer?

key terms

Equality: dignity, respect and rights for all individuals, whatever their differences.

Barriers: anything that blocks the positive attitudes needed in society to value individuals.

Inclusion: individuals are included in services and provisions that reflect their different requirements for care and education and enable a sense of being valued.

Equality

Equality should mean that each person in society is valued for being an individual and that each person has the same rights and access to health care and services. Unfortunately this does not always happen.

In order to achieve **equality** and embrace other cultures and circumstances, we need to dispel negative attitudes and beliefs that are stereotypical. Adult social care workers are committed by the social care code of practice to providing an equal service to all individuals.

We all need to be more flexible in providing a positive and accommodating society for everyone. In other words, we need to break down **barriers.**

Inclusion

It is very important that everyone, whatever their background or ability, has a chance to flourish in our society, to respect others and to be cared for – with the same rights as everyone else.

Equality measures

ACTIVITY

This activity examines your opinions on how equality measures protect workers, patients, residents and other individuals, and include them in a fair and flexible way. Look at the examples of individuals in the first column and the employer's response.

Use the second column to comment on whether you agree or disagree with the employer's response and give your reason. Use the third column to briefly indicate the effect on that person.

Issue	Your response	Effect on employee
Saghir wants to pray twice a day. His boss says this is only possible if other staff agree.		
Mrs Porter wants further training but this takes a full day. She is refused because she works part time.		
Isra wears her hijab to work in the residential care home but has been asked not to because of health and safety.		

Effects of using negative language

It is very important to be aware of the language you use to promote diversity and equality in your day-to-day duties. For example, a person who is called 'stupid' every day may start to believe it is true and their self-worth will decline. This is called a 'self-fulfilling prophecy'.

If people are valued, they are more likely to feel empowered and have more confidence to live the life they wish to lead.

key term

Self-fulfilling prophecy: one's belief in others' perceptions, often viewed as a negative belief.

Being aware of negative language

ACTIVITY

You need to always be aware of the language you use when interacting with those for whom you care.

1. Look at the following list of words and cross out the ones that you think are negative.

intelligent dummy thick ambitious nasty talented beautiful pleasant horrid
idiot pathetic disturbed useless crazy mental ignorant thoughtful
imaginative reliable motivated retarded deficient prejudiced

2. Imagine you receive negative comments from your work colleagues, even though they follow each comment with 'only joking'. How would it make you feel if you didn't share their sense of humour?

3. Now imagine a 21-year-old woman with Down's syndrome. She is happy and manages at home, but has recently started a job in an office. She is going through a transitional period in her life and is noticing that she is excluded by colleagues in a new environment. She now feels 'different' and is valued 'differently'. What effect will this continued perception have on her life?

key terms

Discrimination: actions or attitudes that treat other people less favourably.

Prejudice: an opinion formed without real or sufficient knowledge and understanding. It is based on inaccurate information, irrational feelings, stereotypes, labels and assumptions, with no consideration of the individual.

The potential effects of discrimination

Discrimination is usually seen to have negative outcomes on a person's self-worth or self-esteem and feelings of being valued. As a health and social care worker, you need to take steps to prevent all types of discrimination from occurring or – if it is present – you must help to stop it.

Discrimination results from the inaccurate and unfair judgements made by others as a result of **prejudice**. Prejudice will develop in situations where people are uncertain of others who are different in some way, for example from a different nationality, culture or with different abilities. People deny holding any prejudice and yet they reveal these through their actions towards others and what they say. For example, they may use derogatory language or labels that focus on one aspect of an individual or group, and consider them to be inferior as a result of that difference.

Types of discrimination

ACTIVITY

Research the following types of discrimination using an internet search engine and www.direct.gov.uk.

- ✿ Direct discrimination
- ✿ Positive discrimination
- ✿ Indirect discrimination

When you think you have understood these terms, respond to the following statements by ticking the appropriate box.

	Direct discrimation	Positive discrimination	Indirect discrimination
The housing priority is for the pregnant and homeless.			
Young offenders are offered employment opportunities first.			
Black people needed for work in the community.			
Over-60s to receive free computer training.			
People who are HIV-positive or have hepatitis C are not permitted to live in this country.			
The theatre cannot accommodate wheelchairs.			
Young women required for new hairdressing business.			
Male actor is needed to play 'Hamlet'.			

Anti-discrimination

ACTIVITY

By now you have been challenged to think quite a lot about anti-discriminatory practice. You should have no trouble with the following crossword.

Across

5. Adapting the physical environment is following this model of disability (6)
7. Negative comments towards someone in person (10)
8. Embracing all cultural differences and abilities may promote this (10)
13. To change our own views is to _____ (5)
14. What one likes to do (10)
15. Differences between individuals or groups (9)
16. To offer rights and choices is to _____ (7)

Down

1. The country of one's birth (6)
2. We must challenge this by law (6)
3. Everyone has these legally (6)
4. As if categorising people (12)
6. A barrier to inclusion (9)
9. One's beliefs and customs (7)
10. To have a strong self-esteem, one has to feel this (6)
11. Involving all people and encouraging them to flourish (9)
12. Like a tag (5)

ACTIVITY

Complete the gaps in the following sentences using the words below. This will show that you understand the negative effects of discrimination.

disempowered assumptions bigotry stereotyping
bias unique excluded unfair poor intolerance marginalised
angry motivation vicious diagnosis labelling

✿ _____ means considering people with similar characteristics to be exactly the same and not seeing them as _____. When people favour one side over another, this is called _____.

✿ When people are described in a way that relates only to their appearance, behaviour or _____, then this is referred to as _____. It can lead to others making _____ about them that are _____ and inaccurate.

✿ _____ is when someone continues to hold a prejudiced opinion and an aggressive _____ towards the focus of that prejudice, despite evidence to the contrary.

✿ When discrimination results in people or groups being _____ from belonging or participating in society they are said to be _____.

✿ People who experience negative discrimination often have low self-esteem, and a _____ self-image. They can also feel confused, _____ and depressed. This results in the person feeling _____, which reduces their _____ and achievement and creates a _____ circle that makes the situation worse.

Your questions answered...

What should I do if I see something or hear something that shows discrimination?

You must always report incidents that worry you to your line manager. You need to understand the reporting procedure of the setting and this must be part of your induction when you start work. Please remember that you are accountable for your actions and you must not let poor care practice of any description go unchecked. It may be that further training is needed because staff have a poor understanding, but this is no excuse for bad care practice.

How inclusive practice promotes equality and supports diversity

Inclusive practice is based on viewing and treating the individual as valuable and unique, so they should feel confident about who they are and have their needs recognised and met. They should feel safe, that they belong and are able to participate equally in activities of their choosing. They should be able to express their wishes and have equal access to explore opportunities. When individuals feel included, they are able to take an active role in society and achieve their potential in ways that inspire, motivate and fulfil them.

It is a legal requirement to implement policies and procedures in accordance with equality and diversity law. It is part of your contractual agreement to work within a framework that respects diversity and is fair to all.

Policy statements

ACTIVITY

Think about what the following terms mean to you in a health and social care context. Give an example of a policy statement for each issue to show your understanding of how to promote equality and fairness for staff and support diversity in the sector. An example has been done for you.

Issue	Suggested policy statement
Identity and culture.	All persons employed in the sector will respect the individual identity and cultural beliefs of others with reference to dress code, sexual orientation and customs.
Age and gender.	
Language.	
Religious beliefs.	
Social circumstances and commitments.	

Assessor tip

You will find it easier if you can use examples from your own life and work experience to explain what is meant by diversity, equality, discrimination and inclusion.

Be able to work in an inclusive way

How legislation relating to equality, diversity and discrimination apply to own work role

There have been a number of Acts of Parliament, guidelines and codes of practice to help stamp out discrimination. The Acts that relate to the caring sector include the Care Standards Act 2000, the Human Rights Act 1998 and the Mental Capacity Act 2007.

Revisit these Acts using the internet, to help you with the next activity.

In October 2010, the Equality Act 2010 was introduced to replace with a single act the previous anti-discrimination laws, including the Disability Discrimination Act 1995 and the Race Relations Act 1976. The aim was to make the law simpler and to strengthen protection in some situations.

Under the Equality Act 2010, it is unlawful for individuals to:

❀ be treated badly because they have supported a complaint because of the Act (victimisation)

❀ find the workplace an offensive environment because someone is being bullied or harassed, even if it is not directed at them (harassment)

❀ be treated unfairly because they are associated with a person with a protected characteristic (discrimination by association)

❀ be discriminated against because they are perceived to have a protected characteristic (discrimination by perception).

Acts

ACTIVITY

Use the internet or your own research and knowledge to decide which Act each behaviour breaches, and explain why. You might also want to discuss the statements with colleagues.

Issues	Relevant Act	Reason
A care worker discovered that she had been turned down for promotion because she cares for her mother, who has Alzheimer's disease.		
Mr Ismail is given £5 pocket money every week, but his other £5 is locked away.		

Issues	Relevant Act	Reason
Three families, including nine children, stay in a two-bedroom hostel with not enough facilities for cooking and poor hygienic conditions.		

ACTIVITY

Using the GSCC Code of Practice for Social Care Workers, identify seven standards that relate to working in an inclusive way. For each standard provide at least one example of how you demonstrate this in practice. The first standard has been identified for you.

GSCC Code of Practice standard	Example of how I demonstrate this in my work practice
1. Treating each person as an individual.	
2.	
3.	
4.	
5.	
6.	
7.	

Show interaction with individuals that respects their beliefs, culture, values and preferences

ACTIVITY

Look back at the policy statements activity on page 56. For this activity, give a specific example of how you promote equality and diversity in a health and social care setting with colleagues and individuals in your care. An example has been done for you.

Issue	How I promote equality and diversity with colleagues	How I promote equality and diversity with individuals in my care
Identity and culture.	I respect different dress codes and customs by accepting slightly different (but not discriminatory) ways of working.	I accept that people wear different clothes and have different lifestyles to my own. I can work alongside different cultures, respecting their views and traditions and accommodating these within a care routine, as long as this does not impact the health and well-being of the person or me.
Age and gender.		
Language.		
Religious beliefs.		
Social circumstances and commitments.		

Assessor tip

Use the real work examples from the last two activities as evidence for your portfolio to show how you work in an inclusive way.

key terms

Inclusive practice: this ensures that all individuals are valued and services are centred on each individual's needs and requirements.
Social model of disability: including society in addressing issues of disability in a positive way, for example everyone being able to use sign language so they can communicate with the minority who use sign language.

Equality and inclusion can be demonstrated in practice by encouraging other people to see difference as something to welcome. People have a tendency to overestimate the value of what they have and underestimate the value of what may be gained by doing things differently. Reducing people's fear and anxiety about changing their ideas and accepting things that are different will enable them to broaden their experience. This will increase their understanding, thus reducing their anxiety and encouraging them to be more inclusive.

Promote diversity, equality and inclusion

Actions that model inclusive practice

It is very important to remain positive when working in a health and social care setting. **Inclusive practice** can help banish discrimination and lead to an enrichment of different values.

To do this you must:

* work as a team and seek advice from others
* think about assistive technology and the use of other resources and agencies
* consider the **social model of disability** rather than the **medical model of disability** (see page 62). You can research this in more detail on the internet, to gain a better understanding of applying the principles in practice
* role model inclusive practice because, as an experienced practitioner, colleagues and service users will take their lead from you.

ACTIVITY

Think about the individuals you support and complete the questions to show how you model inclusive practice.

1. Give three examples of how you celebrate the difference of the individuals you support.
   *
   *
   *

2. Give three examples of how you celebrate difference in terms of culture, religion or traditions.
   *
   *
   *

3. Identify three other opportunities you use to promote inclusion and understanding of diversity in your workplace.
   *
   *
   *

How to support others to promote equality and rights

ACTIVITY

There are many aspects to working inclusively. Look at the pictures of individuals who might be in your care.

Meena

Sofia

Harry

Sam

Sulamain

Complete the table describing how a multi-disciplinary team can support the needs of each individual. The first one has been done for you.

The individual	Team intervention
Meena, aged 78, loves to read but now has considerable loss of vision that prevents her from reading text.	Provide the physical resources such as bright lighting, magnifiers and large print. Consult experts and monitor as a team.
Sofia, aged 42, uses a wheelchair to help her to mobilise but before her accident loved to work in her garden.	
Harry, aged 49, has been diagnosed with Pick's disease (a type of dementia) that has severely reduced his concentration levels.	
Sam, aged 21, had an accident in which he sustained a brain injury that has affected his speech.	
Sulamain, aged 25, suffers with extreme anxiety and panic attacks, especially in crowded environments.	

key term

Medical model of disability: this model seeks to 'cure' rather than adapt. The person with the disability is seen as a problem, rather than the barriers that prevent their requirements being met (for example, steps preventing a wheelchair user from entering a building).

How to challenge discrimination in a way that promotes change

It is your duty not to allow any evidence of discrimination to continue, so you must report incidences and practices that you think should change. Staff meetings are regular occurrences and the agenda should include issues of equality and diversity. Raise issues in a positive way and make suggestions for changes in line with legislation. You might want to do this in one-to-one sessions if the issue is more sensitive.

ACTIVITY

Complete the gaps in the following sentences, using the suggestions below in the correct context. Also include your reason (following the word 'because'). The first one has been done for you.

Suggestions

* Invite the public and some health professionals in to talk about issues of concern.
* Invite a health professional to arrange a workshop event to promote healthy foods and exercise.
* Arrange a festival calendar so that religious and cultural special days from around the world can be celebrated.
* Introduce some team games and sports events.
* Explore ways to give more responsibility, independence and decision making.

Willow Day Care Centre caters for 36 residents and attendees aged 19 and upwards, with various ranges of hearing and language impairments. About 40% are resident. Following staff meetings, the manager and the team have made some decisions.

1. Some of the younger residents present with challenging behaviour so the manager has decided to ... <u>explore ways to give more responsibility, independence and decision making</u> ... because ... <u>this tends to increase esteem and self-worth, creating a more positive environment and teamwork efforts.</u>

2. Some of the younger attendees, who just attend during the day, are having problems integrating with residents, so the manager has decided to

   _____

   because _____

   _____

3. The attendees come from a mix of backgrounds and cultures. To promote cultural enrichment, the team will _____

   _____

   because _____

   _____

4. Some community members have complained that the centre can be very noisy at times. It has been decided in a group meeting to _____

_____

because _____

_____

5. Some general health issues, such as obesity and lack of exercise, are concerns among the staff, so it has been decided to _____

_____

because _____

_____

When challenging discrimination, the best outcome would be where the other person can see what they did wrong without feeling belittled. To achieve this, remember to:

* be respectful of the other person and ensure you maintain their privacy and dignity (modelling good practice)
* find out the facts before acting
* do not make assumptions or judgements (there are always two sides to any story or situation)
* listen actively and use this to ask appropriate questions
* reflect the situation back to the person to encourage them to consider how they would feel in the other person's place (create an empathic response)
* encourage the person to consider what they can learn from their empathic response
* ask them what they could do differently in similar circumstances
* check they are all right before you finish talking to them
* follow up at a later date to see if they have put the change into practice
* provide positive feedback when you observe that change in attitude and behaviour (this reinforces the positive behaviour).

Kingfisher residential home

CASE STUDY

Kingfisher has a number of homes for older people in the region but recently two of these have received unsatisfactory reports from the local authorities. One member of staff has been suspended following an investigation in the care home. Mrs Crilly, head of care services, is due to hold a series of meetings to discuss issues.

She has invited residents, carers, friends and relatives for a consultation on services so that they can share their ideas on improving services.

Listed below are the findings for the home.

Issues at Kingfisher Group Residential Home

❀ Food served did not reflect the preferences and cultures of the residents.

❀ Activities provided were infrequent and consisted only of Scrabble or playing cards.

❀ Staff were observed to be using negative language to residents.

❀ Owing to a staff shortage, residents have to fit their care needs around times when the staff overlap.

What would you do? Please make at least one suggestion (per issue) to improve the services in the home.

Assessor tip

Keep note of any occasions when you actively promoted equality, diversity or inclusion or challenged discrimination. These examples will provide good evidence of your understanding and competence for your portfolio.

ARE YOU READY FOR ASSESSMENT?

☑ **Do you know the following:**

☐ **1.** The meanings of diversity, equality and inclusion?

☐ **2.** The effects of discrimination?

☐ **3.** How inclusive practice promotes equality and supports diversity?

☐ **4.** The legislation and codes of practice relating to equality, diversity and discrimination?

☐ **5.** How to challenge discrimination in a way that promotes change?

☑ **Can you do the following:**

☐ **1.** Interact with people in ways that support their beliefs, culture, values and preferences?

☐ **2.** Work in ways that are inclusive and support others to promote equality and rights?

UNIT SHC 34

Principles for implementing duty of care

This unit provides you with the knowledge that will enable you to understand how a duty of care contributes to safe practice. As a carer, you are assumed to have special responsibility to keep people in your care safe. This involves making judgements to determine the safety and well-being of individuals.

As individuals have the right to be empowered to make choices and decisions, you may be faced with dilemmas when people's rights conflict with a duty of care. When this happens, you are expected to take into consideration the reasonableness of any proposed actions. Conflicts and complaints may arise so this unit also addresses how to deal with these.

You will need to be able to:

❀ understand how a duty of care contributes to safe practice

❀ know how to address conflicts or dilemmas that may arise between an individual's rights and the duty of care

❀ respond to complaints.

How a duty of care contributes to safe practice

Have a duty of care in own work role

People needing care often feel vulnerable and so part of your **duty of care** is ensuring this vulnerability is met with safe practice. In other words, you are taking all reasonable precautions to safeguard them within your duty of care.

It is also your duty to carry out your work commitments safely and within accepted guidelines. This applies to the general safety of those in your care when moving about or needing your help with personal care and hygiene.

A duty of care also involves maintaining your professional approach and high standards at all times.

As a health and social care worker, you have a duty of care to all those you work with. This includes service users, their families, your employer and colleagues. Your duty of care to others affects all aspects of your day-to-day work. Your employer also has a duty of care and, in particular, this relates to having appropriate and sufficient policies, procedures and training in place to enable employees to work safely.

Duty of care is also defined through the following.
* Legislation, for example Mental Capacity Act (2005); Control of Substances Hazardous to Health Regulations (COSHH) (2002).
* Organisational policies, for example those relating to health and safety and safeguarding vulnerable people.
* Codes of practice, for example General Social Care Council (GSCC).
* Practice standards, for example Care Quality Commission (CQC) Essential Standards of Quality and Safety.

A failure in your duty of care generally results in individuals being put at unacceptable risk or in actual harm. It is often only at this point that practitioners consider their responsibilities in relation to duty of care. When a practitioner fails in their duty of care, this may result in dismissal and, if appropriate, removal from a professional register. Therefore, understanding your duty of care is essential to good care practice.

The importance of training to maintain a duty of care

In order to deliver safe practice you need to maintain your awareness of current issues to add to your knowledge base. Practices change all the time as a result of new legislation. This means that there are new requirements (and therefore policies) to put in place.

> **key term**
>
> **Duty of care:** a legal obligation to work by set standards, as far as it is reasonable to do so, in order to prevent any harm or danger to those in your care.

ACTIVITY

In Unit SHC 32 'Engage in personal development in health and social core settings', you looked at personal and professional development.

In the left column below are a series of resident histories, and on the right are training updates that would be needed to address the issues raised. Draw a line from the history to the matching training update that will support your knowledge and skills when caring for each resident. It may be appropriate to take part in more than one training update.

Histories	Training updates
Mrs A has recently been admitted and has a number of bruises. She is very nervous when you approach her.	Emergency First Aid at Work
Mr B has congestive cardiac failure and easily gets very breathless. He has also been diagnosed with Alzheimer's disease.	Infection Control and Prevention
Mr C has epilepsy and has not been very stable on medication recently. He may be hiding his medication.	Food Safety and Hygiene
Mrs D has diabetes and often has a low blood sugar reading because she doesn't each much because of a lack of appetite.	Moving and Handling
Mr E has a very weak immune system and is barrier nursed.	Safeguarding of Vulnerable Adults
Mrs F has severe arthritis and can only manage short unsteady steps with her frame to go to the toilet.	Understanding the Safe Handling of Medicines
	Awareness of Dementia and Care
	Diabetes awareness

How a duty of care contributes to the safeguarding or protection of individuals

ACTIVITY

One day you may be in charge of a unit, which means you will be responsible for the safety, well-being and treatments of those in your care.

Imagine that tonight you are going to be in charge of a 15-bed unit for older people. Most are residents requiring no nursing care except medication, but six of the residents are those described in the previous activity.

This is your first night shift and, although you have two assistants with you, you need to know your residents better before they go to sleep.

1. Look at the list of jumbled duties that follow and prioritise them in order of importance, to ensure the residents' safety on your shift. Number the boxes 1 to 10 in the order of what you would do. The first one has been done for you.

Duties	Priority
Hand over to the morning staff.	
When lights are out, ensure all staff remain quiet. Check the resident with anxiety; make tea, if needed.	
Check everyone can access a buzzer in case they need assistance.	
Check everyone is comfortable and fluids are recorded (if routinely recorded) before turning out lights.	
Give everyone a supper-time drink.	
Introduce yourself to each resident and explain the routine, asking if there are any questions or concerns.	1
Check the six identified residents who have health conditions and ask them about any concerns for the night.	
Check that toilets, clinical areas and sluice areas are clean.	
Wash hands and administer medications in accordance with the MAR sheets.	
Periodically check all residents to ensure they are comfortable and safe if mobilising to the toilet.	

2. Now explain why you put each task in the order you chose. What did you think about in order to prioritise them? How does each task relate to your duty of care?

Support networks

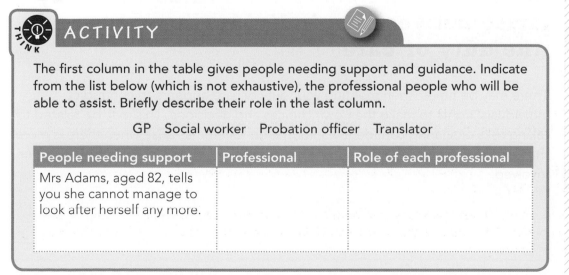

ACTIVITY

The first column in the table gives people needing support and guidance. Indicate from the list below (which is not exhaustive), the professional people who will be able to assist. Briefly describe their role in the last column.

GP   Social worker   Probation officer   Translator

People needing support	Professional	Role of each professional
Mrs Adams, aged 82, tells you she cannot manage to look after herself any more.		

Duty of care

People needing support	Professional	Role of each professional
Daniel, aged 23, has recently left prison but has no confidence.		
Ahmed has just arrived in Britain and can speak very little English.		
Mr Brown is worried that his shortness of breath may be caused by cancer.		

Your questions answered...

When I am busy in a care setting, how can I give a proper duty of care?

If you do not adhere to standards that safeguard those in your care you are in breach of your contract and the outcome may well be that someone becomes very ill or has an accident. You are accountable for your actions to keep individuals safe; you could lose your job and cause the setting to close down if you ignore safeguarding duties.

Task-orientated approaches are not good care routines and can lead to more serious issues developing.

Address conflicts or dilemmas that may arise between an individual's rights and the duty of care

There may be times when meeting your duty of care appears to contradict individuals' rights to make their own choices and decisions. This may be related to taking risks or sharing confidential information. Dilemmas arise when there is more than one course of action but none will meet the needs and/or wishes of everyone involved.

How dilemmas might be managed

 ACTIVITY

A **potential dilemma** may arise when individuals do not wish to comply with the care you want to give them. They might refuse treatment or simply do not know about their options. Look at the cases below and comment on what you think the potential dilemma is and give your response to avoid a dilemma. An example has been done for you.

Issue	What is the potential dilemma?	Your response
Ray refuses to take his epilepsy medication.	Ray has a right to refuse medication but I have a duty of care to ensure he does not come to harm through not taking his medication as prescribed.	I would give Ray some information about the type of medication he requires. I would also tell him that I need to know why he refuses to take his medication.
Caroline is struggling with her diabetes and is depressed.		
Christian needs an eye operation and is worried about the risks.		
Mrs Cole is unable to see well but says she will not go into a home for the blind.		
Aria has special needs. She asks you not to tell her mother that she is pregnant.		

One important factor to consider when faced with dilemmas about balancing rights and risks is the individual's capacity to make an informed decision: their ability to think and reason sufficiently to reach a decision. A lack of capacity to make informed decisions may be temporary (owing to an accident or having anaesthetic) or permanent (because of an inherited or acquired condition, or failing health). If the situation is permanent, someone may have been appointed to act on the individual's behalf and in their best interests. If the lack of capacity is not confirmed or is temporary, you have a duty of care to act in the individual's best interests. That may involve seeking advice and support to enable an objective view of the dilemma before reaching a decision.

Where to get additional support and advice about conflicts and dilemmas

An important way to manage these conflicts and dilemmas is to seek support and advice from others. This enables you and the individual to look at the situation from different perspectives. Standards, policies and procedures can also offer guidance.

ACTIVITY

Imagine that you have tried your best to negotiate and advise the people who appear in the previous activity. Despite your best efforts they are not choosing to do what you think they should do for their health and well-being.

1. Suggest a source to give you help and support in each case. What can you do to ensure this is accessed by the individuals and complied with? The first one has been done for you.

Dilemmas	Sources of support and how I would monitor actions
Ray refuses to take his epilepsy medication.	My line manager, the GP and/or pharmacist. Later visits should reveal if Ray is maintaining his medication regime.
Caroline is struggling with her diabetes and is depressed.	
Christian needs an eye operation and is worried about the risks.	
Mrs Cole is unable to see well but says she will not go into a home for the blind.	
Aria has special needs. She asks you not to tell her mother that she is pregnant.	

2. Briefly describe the effects on the independence, health, safety and well-being of two of these individuals if nothing was done to support them.

ACTIVITY

List four external agencies and four organisational policies and procedures that you could refer to for advice and guidance regarding your duty of care.

✿

✿

✿

✿

✿

✿

✿

✿

Assessor tip

Keep a record of any occasions when you have accessed support to resolve duty of care dilemmas as this will be useful when explaining how to manage and resolve dilemmas.

Know how to respond to complaints

Complaints

If the way you care for and support individuals conflicts with their rights, they may make a complaint. Complaints can be made, and dealt with, formally or informally.

When an issue first arises, it helps to talk, and talking through a situation can help identify the problem and how it can be resolved to everyone's satisfaction.

A complaint about a service has to be addressed positively. Complaints provide feedback on the quality and performance of a service, which can be helpful in improving things and increasing user satisfaction and safety.

However, bearing in mind your duty to safeguard people, you must use a **risk assessment** process to determine the effect on health, safety and welfare.

You will come across risk assessment many times, in health and safety situations and person-centred care approaches. Risk assessing is a legal requirement of your practice.

A risk assessment involves:

❀ the hazards and associated risks
❀ deciding who might be harmed and how
❀ evaluating the risks to determine what will reduce them
❀ recording the findings
❀ monitoring, reviewing and revising.

Ada

CASE STUDY

Ada, aged 86, is trying to live independently but is struggling with washing herself as she can no longer take a bath.

Her daughter, Christine, has complained that her mother's care worker only has 15 minutes with her twice a day, and the only time she bathed her it was so rushed that Ada has refused to wash since. The relationship with the carer is poor because she is task-orientated.

Using the risk assessment steps above, plan your meeting with Ada and Christine. Briefly indicate your response.

Ada has a complaint

1. Why is this conflict a potential risk to health, safety and welfare? (Identify the potential risk.)

2. How severe is this risk? (Analyse.)

3. What steps or actions could be taken to minimise the risk? (Reduce the likelihood of risks occurring.)

4. How will you monitor the steps or actions? (Monitor the outcomes.)

5. When will you review the effectiveness of this action? (Realistic timescales for review.)

6. In summary, what should you highlight to the mother and her daughter?

Remember that this procedure needs to be considered, discussed and agreed with both women.

The agreed procedures for handling complaints

Every organisation in the sector has a complaints procedure and part of your induction is to become familiar with the one for your organisation.

ACTIVITY

Read the following examples of procedures and tick whether you think they are true or false.

TRUE/FALSE

- ❀ The complainant has to write everything down.
- ❀ The carer must follow the grievance policy.
- ❀ The carer must write down the complaint in the words of the complainant.
- ❀ Effective listening skills are needed.
- ❀ Summarising and reflecting are important so that facts are accurate.
- ❀ Use risk assessment steps to try to reach a consensus for the way forward.
- ❀ You do not need to add your name, date or signature to reports.
- ❀ At your level, you do not get involved in complaints.
- ❀ Referral to other professionals may be required.
- ❀ You must not tell the complainant that other people will be involved.

Although you may have a busy workload, any complaint is of great importance to the person who makes it. A speedy response may not be possible, but that is exactly what the person will be looking for; the longer frustrations continue, the more anxious that person will become, which could compromise health, safety and welfare. Keep them informed at all stages.

When responding to a complaint, it is important to:
- ❀ be respectful, polite and courteous
- ❀ provide privacy and maintain confidentiality, for example by sitting down together in a private place
- ❀ concentrate on the individual and be mindful of your body language
- ❀ listen carefully to what is being said
- ❀ keep calm, speak calmly and quietly as this will reduce the individual's heightened emotional state
- ❀ acknowledge their complaint without being defensive
- ❀ not pre-judge the situation.

Assessor tip

Remember, it is important when explaining to your assessor how to respond to a complaint to include how you would behave towards the other person, as well as the correct policy and procedure.

Performance and procedures

ACTIVITY

THINK

This activity tries to sum up your responsibilities and outlines the basic process for handling complaints.

1. Rearrange the following anagrams into their proper words; they all relate to 'duty of care'.

    shrigt   yigindt   seeptcr   vitaldindiyui   deepdennicen   yapivcr   icehoc

2. Complete the gaps in the following sentences by using the words above.

    ✿ Always remember that people have _____ and should be treated with _____ and _____.

    ✿ Every day, recognise their _____ by promoting _____.

    ✿ Always ensure _____ and _____ during personalised care routines.

3. Complete the gaps in the following sentences by using the words below.

    acknowledge   solution   reassurance   investigated   steps   line manager   listening   complaint

    ✿ If there is a _____, always _____ this by _____ carefully and writing down the _____ you took to improve the situation.

    ✿ Inform your _____ _____ as soon as possible but give _____ that the complaint will be _____.

    ✿ A _____ will be sought by following policy and procedures.

ARE YOU READY FOR ASSESSMENT?

☑ **Do you know the following:**

☐ **1.** What 'duty of care' means in your work role?

☐ **2.** How duty of care contributes to safeguarding or protecting individuals?

☐ **3.** The potential conflicts or dilemmas that can arise between duty of care and individual rights?

☐ **4.** How to manage the risks associated with these conflicts or dilemmas?

☐ **5.** The additional support and advice available to resolve duty of care conflicts and dilemmas?

☐ **6.** How to respond to complaints using agreed procedures?

☐ **7.** The man points of the organisation's agreed complaints procedure?

UNIT HSC 024

Principles of safeguarding and protection in health and social care

There is no excuse for abuse. It is illegal and everyone has the right to be free from abuse. People who use health and social care services are vulnerable, and often at risk of abuse. As a health and social care worker, your role is to safeguard and protect the people you care for and support.

This unit gives you an opportunity to demonstrate that you understand different types of abuse, what makes a person particularly vulnerable to abuse and what you must do when you suspect, or someone alleges, that it is taking place.

You will need to be able to:
* recognise the signs of abuse
* respond to suspected or alleged abuse
* understand the national and local context of safeguarding and protection from abuse
* understand ways to reduce the likelihood of abuse
* recognise and report unsafe practices.

Recognise the signs of abuse

To abuse is to violate or deprive someone of their rights. There are different types of abuse. You need to know what they are, how to recognise them and be aware of what can make people especially vulnerable.

Different types of abuse

ASK

ACTIVITY

Use a dictionary or an internet search engine to define the different types of abuse and complete the spider diagram.

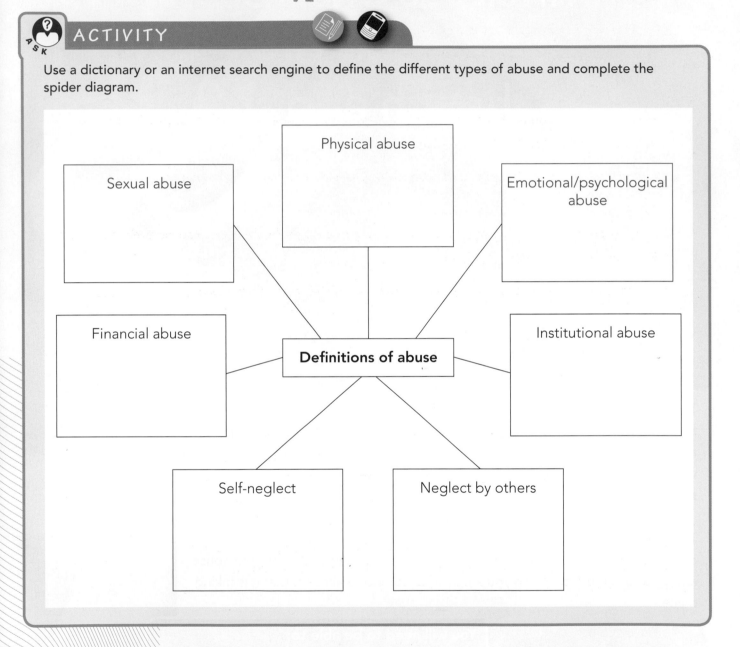

Physical abuse

Sexual abuse

Emotional/psychological abuse

Financial abuse

Definitions of abuse

Institutional abuse

Self-neglect

Neglect by others

Examples of the different types of abuse

Sometimes abuse is very obvious, such as someone beating a partner or treating an older person disrespectfully. However, abuse can be more subtle and may not always be easy to detect. In these cases it may go undetected for years. The next activity gives you some examples to think about.

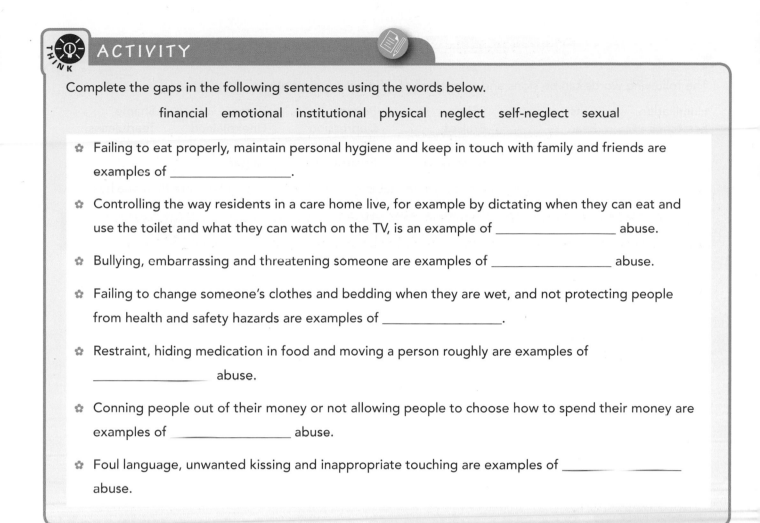

ACTIVITY

Complete the gaps in the following sentences using the words below.

financial   emotional   institutional   physical   neglect   self-neglect   sexual

✿ Failing to eat properly, maintain personal hygiene and keep in touch with family and friends are examples of _____.

✿ Controlling the way residents in a care home live, for example by dictating when they can eat and use the toilet and what they can watch on the TV, is an example of _____ abuse.

✿ Bullying, embarrassing and threatening someone are examples of _____ abuse.

✿ Failing to change someone's clothes and bedding when they are wet, and not protecting people from health and safety hazards are examples of _____.

✿ Restraint, hiding medication in food and moving a person roughly are examples of _____ abuse.

✿ Conning people out of their money or not allowing people to choose how to spend their money are examples of _____ abuse.

✿ Foul language, unwanted kissing and inappropriate touching are examples of _____ abuse.

The signs and symptoms of abuse

Signs are things that can be seen, heard and felt by touch. Signs of good health include physical signs such as a healthy skin colour, with blood pressure and pulse rates that fall within normal boundaries. There are also signs of emotional and psychological health that show if the individual is contented with life, generally happy and not depressed or withdrawn.

Symptoms are signs that generally cannot be seen, heard or felt by other people. They are the feelings that people have. Negative feelings can be noted in a person's body language and facial expressions.

ACTIVITY

The following words can be signs and symptoms of different types of abuse.

Humiliation	Cuts	STIs	Poverty	Burns	Shame
Scratches	Fear	Bruises	Depression	Unexplained	Tearfulness
Anxiety	Withdrawal	Soiling	Emaciation	pregnancy	Despair
Bleeding	Debt	Loneliness	Frustration	Anger	

List each word under the appropriate heading in the table below. They may fit under more than one heading.

Physical abuse	Sexual abuse	Emotional abuse	Financial abuse	Institutional abuse	Neglect and self-neglect

Reasons why some people are more vulnerable to abuse

Some people are more vulnerable to abuse than others. Vulnerability depends on the individual and the **setting** or situation in which they live. For example, someone with learning difficulties may be vulnerable because they may not have the experience to deal with a **perpetrator**. An older person living with their family may be vulnerable because family members may not have the necessary skills and qualities to care for them appropriately.

ACTIVITY

As you know, bullying is a form of abuse.

Think now about situations where you might have noticed bullying.

1. Why do you think these incidents occurred?

2. In your view, what feelings did the perpetrator experience?

3. What kind of response from the person being bullied might lead to further bullying?

4. What measures would stop the bullying?

What have I done wrong?

ACTIVITY

Complete the table to show that you understand why different groups of people are vulnerable to abuse. An example has been done for you.

Groups of people	Why these groups of people are vulnerable to abuse
Older people.	They may not have the physical strength or confidence to challenge someone who abuses or neglects them.
People with learning difficulties.	
People with physical disabilities.	
People with personal care needs.	

Groups of people	Why these groups of people are vulnerable to abuse
People living alone.	
People with mental health problems.	

Know how to respond to suspected or alleged abuse

What to do if you suspect that someone is being abused

ACTIVITY

The following are potential abuse cases. Describe the possible signs and symptoms for each individual.

1. Mrs Reilly's daughter is seen to be treating her mother roughly when she puts her in her wheelchair, and is always impatient and shouting at her.

2. Mr Epping is unable to cook for himself since his fall three weeks ago but no one has supported him.

3. Molly is 35 and has mental health issues. Today she refuses to go out shopping with a certain carer.

If you suspect that someone is being abused, for example if you observe an unexplained injury or changes in someone's behaviour that cause you concern, doing nothing is not an option. Don't collude with colleagues involved or make the situation worse by covering it up. Similarly, if someone tells you they are concerned for another person's safety you must do something about it. However, you must go about it in the right way, and not act or make promises without careful thought. You also need to make sure the person is safe before leaving them to report the situation. Your organisation will have a procedure that tells you how to deal with suspicions of abuse, but in general:

* **report** your concerns to your manager, verbally and in writing
* **never** make a promise regarding an allegation of abuse
* **don't** investigate or question anyone yourself.

Your manager must respond to your concerns and let you know the outcome of their enquiries.

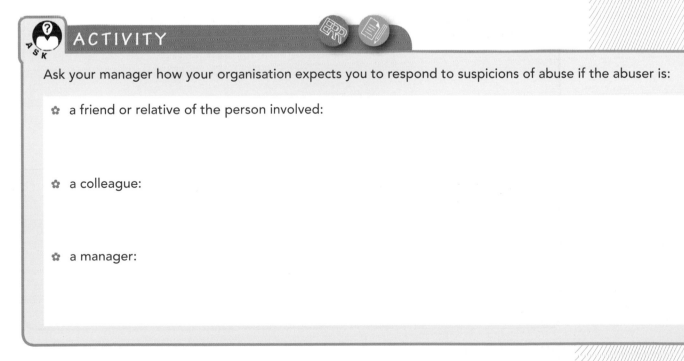

ACTIVITY

Ask your manager how your organisation expects you to respond to suspicions of abuse if the abuser is:

* a friend or relative of the person involved:

* a colleague:

* a manager:

❀ you:

❀ anyone else:

What to do if someone tells you they are being abused

An effective health and social care worker is someone to whom individuals turn to and trust. If you are such a person, there may be times when someone will **allege** that abuse is taking place. If this happens, you must follow your organisation's procedure and you should expect to be kept informed about the result of enquiries.

ACTIVITY

Ask your manager how your organisation expects you to deal with allegations of abuse. Make notes below about what you are told.

ACTIVITY

Complete the gaps in the following sentences using the words below. This will show that you know how to respond to an allegation of abuse.

calm   interrupt   judgemental   listen   record   secret   seriously

✿ _____ carefully to what the person tells you.

✿ Take what they say _____.

✿ Keep _____ and don't be _____.

✿ Don't _____ them, in other words, don't ask lots of questions. Just let them tell you what they want to say.

✿ Explain that you cannot keep what they've told you a _____. You need to get help from your manager, but reassure them that you won't tell anyone else. Maintain their trust in you.

✿ Make a written _____ of what they tell you, using their own words. Sign and date the record and speak with your manager without delay.

Mrs Clarke

CASE STUDY

Mrs Clarke attends the luncheon club where you are a support worker. She lives on her own and enjoys the company, especially yours. One day she tells you very quietly that she can't come any more because she doesn't have enough money and, anyway, her daughter can't understand why she can't eat at home because it's cheaper. She shows you her cheque book, which is empty of cheques but the stubs have not been completed. She cannot find the card she uses to withdraw her pension from the post office. With much anxiety, she tells you that her daughter has been using her cheque book and has taken her bank card but asks you to say nothing about this to anyone else as she's sure things will sort themselves out.

1. What type of abuse is happening here?

2. What should you do?

Responding to an allegation of abuse

Making sure that evidence of abuse is preserved

Your questions answered...

Something dreadful happened a couple of days ago at the residential care home where I work — an intruder got in and sexually assaulted one of the female residents. I was the first person to discover the resident after the assault and was so shocked at the time that I don't think I dealt with the situation properly. In fact, the police were quite impatient with me; they said I should have preserved the evidence of abuse. I'm not sure what this means. Can you please help?

Your workplace should have a procedure in the event that such a trauma takes place, but the three golden rules for preserving evidence are:

* don't move anything
* don't touch anything
* don't throw anything away.

Suspicion and allegations of abuse have to be investigated by the police, so all associated evidence must be preserved. This includes footprints, fingerprints and body fluids that the perpetrator may have left behind; CCTV footage; records about, for example, the victim's clothing and the physical and emotional condition of the person who has been abused at the time when the abuse was discovered, as well as of any first aid that was given.

Thelma

CASE STUDY

Thelma is a resident at a home for people with learning difficulties. It's lunchtime but Thelma hasn't arrived in the dining room. You go to her room and find her crouched on the floor, extremely distressed and her clothes dishevelled. She manages to tell you that someone has interfered with her, and you can see that her pants are under a chair and that she is bleeding.

1. What evidence would be needed to investigate whether abuse has taken place?

2. What must you do to ensure that this evidence is preserved?

The national and local context of safeguarding and protection from abuse

National policies and local systems that relate to safeguarding and protection from abuse

National policies are produced by the government in response to nationally important issues. National policies that relate to safeguarding and protection from abuse, for example Safeguarding Adults (2005), aim to ensure that there is a broad range of services in place to safeguard and protect vulnerable adults.

ACTIVITY

Use an internet search engine to check out examples of national policies that relate to safeguarding and protecting people from abuse. Use your findings to complete the spider diagram.

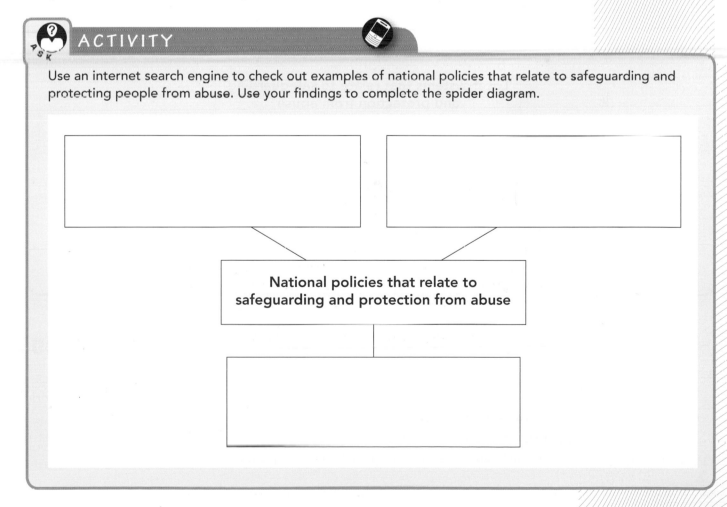

National policies that relate to safeguarding and protection from abuse

key terms

Agency: an organisation that provides a particular service.
Multi-agency working: where a number of different agencies work together with a common goal.

Local systems that relate to safeguarding and protection from abuse are the arrangements for safeguarding and protecting vulnerable people in a locality. They bring together a range of different **agencies**, for example:

✿ local health authorities

✿ local police services

✿ local authority social services and education departments

✿ private organisations and charities that support vulnerable adults within a local authority area.

The different agencies work together to safeguard and protect vulnerable people from abuse. This is known as **multi-agency working**, and the policies and procedures that underpin their work are a response to government policies and the needs of local people.

ACTIVITY

Use an internet search engine to check out examples of systems within your local authority area that relate to safeguarding and protecting people from abuse. Use your findings to complete the spider diagram.

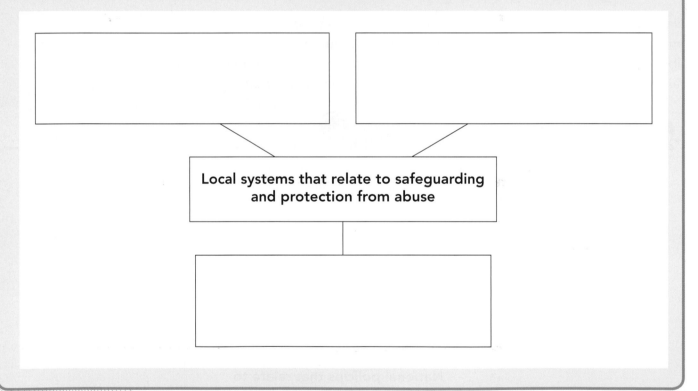

The roles of different agencies in safeguarding and protecting people from abuse

If someone is at risk of abuse, workers from different agencies work with them and each other to minimise or eliminate the risk. For their work to be successful, all workers must have a clear understanding of their own and each other's roles, and must carry out their role as agreed and as expected.

ACTIVITY

Safeguarding vulnerable people depends on effective and coordinated joint working between different agencies. Complete the table to show your understanding of the roles of five different agencies in safeguarding and protecting vulnerable people from abuse. The first one has been done for you.

Agency	Roles in safeguarding and protecting vulnerable adults
CQC (Care Quality Commission).	Under the Health and Social Care Act 2008, the CQC is an agency that makes sure health and social care providers meet government standards of quality and safety. The most recent are the 16 Essential Standards, of which five outcomes are related to the safety of people using services.
Local authority social services/safeguarding boards.	
The police.	
Local neighbourhood community schemes.	
Age UK (formerly Age Concern).	

Reports into serious failures to protect people from abuse

The media continue to report serious failures in protecting people from abuse. These failures are usually the result of poor communication between the different agencies, a lack of understanding about work roles and conflict between workers. Government-led inquiries and reports often result from complaints made by the general public or through **whistle-blowing** procedures.

ACTIVITY

Use an internet search engine to research three cases of serious failure to protect vulnerable adults. Try searching for 'Serious failures to protect vulnerable adults from abuse.'

Which three cases did you research?

1.

2.

3.

What did the courts or inquiry reports say caused the failures?

1.

2.

3.

Assessor tip

Make sure you read through your organisation's policies and procedures prior to assessment. Your assessor will expect you to be able to explain how national policies and reports into serious failures have influenced local and organisational safeguarding procedures. This information is often found in the introduction to the procedures or explained during training.

Information and advice about your role in safeguarding and protecting people from abuse

There are many sources of information and advice about your role in safeguarding and protecting the people you care for and support. There is no excuse for abuse, so make sure you access information and advice in the event that you have any concerns about your role.

ACTIVITY

Complete the following wordsearch to show that you know where to go for information and advice about your role in safeguarding and protecting the people you care for and support.

```
O T H E R A G E N C I E S D Y G E C N O S L M O V
N D I C B H Z P C O D E S O F P R A C T I C E O R
F I J V N Q H Y I B Q H V N W W D H X Z K P K F C
E V C P I Q B O T P V B G D T X B W Q S X M D U J
C G T F O F C L U J K V U G I R I S Q J C T P E I
X A E C Q L V Y G U I D A N C E D O C U M E N T S
T C Q P M E I F A Z G E A M A N A G E M E N T X T
S X G Z G G X C E M O P G B N E K W W R V V O H D
J O B D E S C R I P T I O N S I S S E Y A O F K T
K D T Y O W G X Z E C O L L E A G U E S L C F L A
N B Y P X M A M B F S R A I L C A I X J X Q H U Z
X N Y L O L G B Q Q N B U Y V X C Q V T E F D P Z
N W K Y C T P R O C E D U R E S N H U K W I G Q A
```

policies   procedures   colleagues   management   job descriptions
codes of practice   other agencies   guidance documents

Reducing the likelihood of abuse

Working with person-centred values

Working with person-centred values shows that you value the people you care for and support, and you view them as active partners in their care, not just **passive** recipients of care. As a result, you pay greater attention to the way you provide care and support, which in turn reduces the risk of abuse and neglect.

key term

Passive: inactive; dependent on others; unwilling to make decisions and choices.

Encouraging active participation

Working in ways that recognise individuals' rights to be involved in every aspect of their life and that encourage independence is an important part of protecting them from harm or abuse. When ways of working are built around the individual being an active participant in their care and support, rather than a passive recipient, they will be involved in decision making, listened to and, therefore, feel more able to speak out when they are being treated unfairly or in ways that are harmful or abusive.

Promoting choice and rights

In health and social care settings where care workers actively promote individual choice and rights, the potential for abuse is reduced. This approach encourages a culture of listening and openness. When these exist, people feel more able to express their views and concerns, which makes it more difficult for potential abusers to hide their actions.

ACTIVITY

Complete the gaps in the following sentences using the words below. This will show that you understand the values that are central to a person-centred approach

dignity   independence   individuals   partnership   privacy   respect

Person-centred care means that:

* I must treat the people I care for and support with _____ and as _____.

* I must promote and support their rights to choice and _____.

* I must help maintain their _____ and _____.

* I must encourage them to work with me in _____.

ACTIVITY

Think of five examples to show how you actively promote individual rights and choices in your workplace, and how your actions reduce the likelihood of abuse.

*

Assessor tip

Write a case study to demonstrate how you work in a person-centred way and how this has encouraged active participation while promoting choice and rights. This would be a good source of portfolio evidence.

Accessible complaints procedures

Complaints are a good way of monitoring how well services are provided and of identifying where there are weaknesses, for example the potential for abuse and neglect. An accessible complaints procedure, such as one which is simple to follow and openly available, is a good way of reducing the likelihood of abuse as this encourages people to raise their concerns and indicates that the organisation will respond to those concerns rather than ignore them. You can read about accessible complaints procedures in Unit SHC 34 'Principles for implementing duty of care'.

Recognise and report unsafe practices

Unsafe practices that can affect the well-being of people you care for and support

Unsafe practice may be considered to be any practice that puts others at an unacceptable risk of harm or abuse. Abuse is caused by:

* poor work practices, such as those that cause pain and suffering, do not meet people's needs and do not promote person-centred values, choice and rights
* resource and operational difficulties, such as lack of training, lack of time, lack of and/or poorly maintained equipment, lack of appropriate procedures, lack of supervision and security issues that increase the risk of intruders.

ACTIVITY

Imagine that you have been asked to support a new worker, Aysan. Look at the issues and concerns that may arise with regard to the quality and safety of Aysan's work; these are listed in the second column. Complete the last column to show your knowledge and current expertise. What advice would you give to Aysan?

Work activity	Aysan's concerns	Resource, operational difficulties or outside agencies that you could advise her about that will ensure safety
Helping Mrs J to have a bath.	Mrs J has put on weight recently and Aysan says she is too small to manage her and Mrs J might slip or fall.	
Assisting with dressing Mr A, who has a lot of pain.	Aysan fears dressing Mr A because Mr A's movements are stiff and he is often in agony. She fears that he will strain a muscle or suffer a fracture if she is not gentle enough.	
Mrs L has an annexe in the grounds but is frightened of intruders.	Aysan will work a night duty soon and wonders how she will ensure the security of the three annexe buildings.	

What to do if you identify unsafe practices

Unsafe practices must never be ignored. There is no excuse for allowing them to continue. All health and social care organisations should have a procedure for reporting unsafe practices.

Jim

CASE STUDY

Jim is the handyman at Carefree Residential Care Home. He sees a lot of things that other staff are too busy or too careless to notice, such as medication left lying around, incomplete entries in the visitors' book, alcohol rub containers left empty for days at a time, spillages on floors, overflowing waste receptacles and staff having to carry out activities for which he knows they're not qualified. In addition, one or two of the staff are not in good health. As for his work, some of the equipment he uses is either very old or in need of a service. However, he doesn't say anything – he gets paid every week and that's all he's worried about.

1. How might these examples of bad practice be construed as abuse? The first one has been done for you.

✿ Medication left lying around:
Health hazard. Physical abuse.

✿ Incomplete entries in the visitors' book:

✿ Alcohol rub containers left empty for days at a time:

✿ Spillages on floors:

Don't ignore unsafe practices

✿ Overflowing waste receptacles:

✿ Staff having to carry out activities for which they're not qualified:

✿ Staff not in good health:

✿ Equipment that is old or in need of a service:

✿ The casual, careless attitude of staff:

✿ Staff are too busy:

2. Jim is in a good position to identify bad practice, in himself as well as in others. How do you think he should respond? Give reasons for your answers.

What to do if you report abuse or unsafe practice and nothing is done in response

You should be kept informed about how reports of abuse and unsafe practice are dealt with. However, if your employer does nothing in response to your report, you need to speak to a higher authority, such as the organisation that regulates the service you provide. You might even want to blow the whistle on your employer (become a whistle-blower).

 **ACTIVITY**

1. What organisation regulates the service you provide?

2. What other external agencies could you approach for advice and support?

 **ACTIVITY**

Use an internet search engine to find out about whistle-blowing. For example, when should you do this? Who can you talk to or blow the whistle to? What law protects whistle-blowers? What criteria do whistle-blowers have to meet in order to be protected by the law?

Assessor tip

Find out about the whistle-blowing or confidential reporting policies and procedures so you are able to explain these to your assessor.

ARE YOU READY FOR ASSESSMENT?

☑ **Do you know the following:**

☐ **1.** The definitions of the different types of abuse?

☐ **2.** The signs and symptoms of each type of abuse?

☐ **3.** The factors that make an individual more vulnerable to abuse?

☐ **4.** The actions to take and not to take if you suspect abuse?

☐ **5.** The actions to take and not to take if a person alleges abuse?

☐ **6.** How to make sure no evidence is lost or contaminated?

☐ **7.** The national, local and organisational safeguarding policies and procedures?

☐ **8.** The roles of different agencies involved in safeguarding vulnerable people?

☐ **9.** How inquiry reports into failures in practice affect safeguarding procedures?

☐ **10.** Sources of information and advice about your role in safeguarding procedures?

☐ **11.** How to reduce the likelihood of abuse through having an accessible complaints procedure and working in a person-centred way, which encourages active participation and promotes individual choice and rights?

☐ **12.** The effect unsafe practices may have on the well-being of individuals?

☐ **13.** How to identify unsafe practices?

☐ **14.** The action to take if you identify unsafe practices?

☐ **15.** The action to take when no response occurs when suspected abuse or unsafe practices have been reported?

UNIT HSC 025

The role of the health and social care worker

People who have a passion for working in health and social care play a valuable and important role. Their skills, personal qualities and dedication to providing quality care and support contribute enormously to the health, safety and well-being of the most vulnerable people in society.

This chapter aims to provide you with the knowledge and skills you need to become a safe and effective health and social care worker, to work in ways that are agreed with your employer and work in partnership with others.

You will need to be able to:
- ❀ understand working relationships in health and social care
- ❀ understand the agreed ways of working
- ❀ work in partnership with others.

Working relationships in health and social care

The difference between a working relationship and a personal relationship

A relationship is a connection between people. Good relationships are very important as they offer companionship, support, a sense of belonging and a feeling of being valued and cared for.

There are two main types of relationship.

* Personal relationships, for example, family, friendships and sexual relationships. Since personal relationships involve emotions, their breakdown leaves people feeling hurt and betrayed.

* Working relationships, for example the relationships you have with your colleagues and the people you care for and support. Working relationships allow you to be purposeful in your work, to give and receive trust and respect, and to leave work behind when you go home at the end of a shift. They also protect you by giving you **professional boundaries**.

> **key term**
>
> **Professional boundaries:** limits that tell you what you can and cannot do in your job role.

 ACTIVITY

Read the following scenarios about relationships and then answer the questions below.

* Lena is a care worker in a day centre where her long-term friend, Bessie, has been referred for support. They have been there for each other through good times and bad until recently, when Bessie heard that Lena had been talking about her behind her back, criticising her and spreading hurtful and false rumours.

Friend or professional?

* Tom has multiple sclerosis and Carla is his support worker. Recently Tom asked Carla if she would help him have a bath. Giving baths is not part of Carla's job role but because they've known each other for such a long time, Carla agreed to help. They ended up kissing.

* Abdul has recently moved into a residential care home. Bob, a care worker at the home, tells Abdul that he knows exactly what his residents are thinking and what they need. Abdul shouldn't worry because if he wants anything at any time of the day or night, Bob will be there to do it for him. He says he is Abdul's friend.

1. How would you describe the relationships in each scenario?

2. What problems do you anticipate in the abilities of Lena, Carla and Bob to provide professional care and support?

 ACTIVITY

Effective working relationships require:

* clear communication
* honesty
* respect
* cooperation
* trust
* reliability
* shared goals.

Look again at the previous activity and think about which of the above factors are missing from the working relationships.

1. Lena and Bessie:

2. Carla and Tom:

3. Abdul and Bob:

Different working relationships in health and social care settings

Care work involves partnership working or teamwork with a wide range of people.

ACTIVITY

Think about two colleagues you work with. For each person, describe how you work with them and what sort of relationship you have with them as a result. An example is given for you.

I work with people with mental health issues and I regularly participate in meetings when I am asked my opinion of people's progress towards independence. A key person who attends these meetings is the social worker of four of the residents. He is very interested in how I work with the residents and the observations I make. I respond to this enthusiasm by logging activities that I have designed and how I help them to gain confidence and manage their activities of daily living. He supports me by listening to the outcomes and suggesting other tactics where some may not be successful.

✿

✿

Agreed ways of working

You need to be able to work in ways that are agreed with your employer and written into your job role.

Why you should adhere to the agreed scope of your job role

The scope of your job role is the sum of everything you have to do to get your job done. It describes what activities you need to do, how, when, where and who with, and is based on criteria such as your age, capabilities, experience and training. It's important that you work within the scope of your job role because if you don't, you may jeopardise the health, safety and well-being of many people.

ACTIVITY

Complete the following table to show that you understand why it is important to adhere to the agreed scope of your job.

Brief description of three of your day-to-day activities	What could happen if you didn't carry out these activities as agreed?

Accessing full and up-to-date details of agreed ways of working

Agreed ways of working include:

* formal procedures, which are prescribed, rigid ways of working that you are legally obliged to follow exactly as written
* less formal procedures, which allow for flexibility of working in situations where rigid procedures will not meet individual needs.

Agreed ways of working with the people you care for and support need to be updated frequently, to take account of changes in, for example, their health and social care needs, medical advances and legislation.

ACTIVITY

Think about one of your day-to-day work activities.

1. What agreed ways of working tell you how to do this activity? For example, moving and handling procedures tell you how to help someone to move from a bed to a chair.

2. If you need reminding about how to do the activity, where can you find the agreed ways of working?

3. In what situations would these agreed ways of working need to be updated?

4. How do you know that an agreed way of working is up to date?

5. What could happen if you carried out this activity using an out-of-date technique?

Follow agreed ways of working

Implement agreed ways of working

You have a legal and a moral responsibility to follow agreed ways of working, as a failure to do so could jeopardise the health, safety and well-being of everyone concerned. For the same reason, you must never carry out any activity that has not been agreed and written into your job role.

ACTIVITY

Keep a diary for a week to describe four or five of your day-to-day activities and how you make sure that you follow agreed ways of working. Ask a senior colleague to confirm that you follow agreed ways of working by initialling each entry.

Lisa

CASE STUDY

Lisa is a care support worker in a day care setting for adults with learning difficulties. She is still in training but is able to assist her colleagues in most aspects of the work, such as making sure the clients are safe, happy and stimulated. One thing she has not been trained to do is support people who have been abused. However, one of the clients, Penny, has told her that she does not want to go home because her mum hurts her. Lisa can see bruises on Penny's upper arms. When Penny's mother arrives to take her home, Lisa accuses her of physical abuse in front of everyone and threatens to call the police.

1. Is Lisa implementing agreed ways of working? Explain your answer.

2. What could be the result of Lisa's behaviour for:
❀ Lisa?

❀ Penny?

Agreed ways of working?

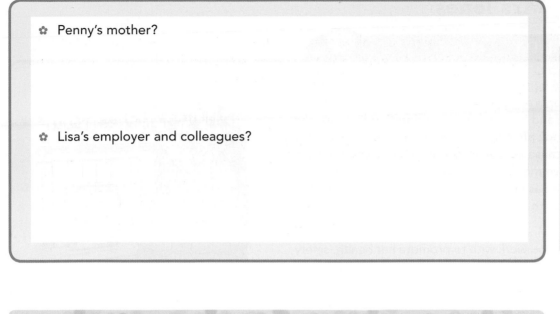

* Penny's mother?

* Lisa's employer and colleagues?

Working in partnership with others

The importance of working in partnership with others

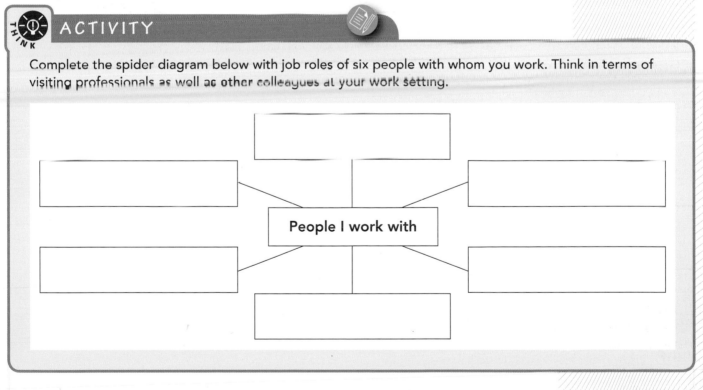

ACTIVITY

Complete the spider diagram below with job roles of six people with whom you work. Think in terms of visiting professionals as well as other colleagues at your work setting.

People I work with

Teamwork

When working in health and social care, teamwork or partnership is very important. It enables people with different skills and qualities to come together to meet all of an individual's needs. Your work with the people you care for and support is essential but they may have additional needs that you or your organisation cannot meet.

Mrs Jones

CASE STUDY

Mrs Jones, who is in her late 80s, lives alone in her bungalow. Her memory is deteriorating, she has mobility problems that put her at risk of falling and her health is deteriorating because she finds it difficult to look after herself and her home properly. She is also very lonely because her family is not close by and her friends are either dead, have moved to live with their family or are in residential care. She has always been a devout Roman Catholic but can no longer go to church.

Imagine that you are Mrs Jones' key worker. What five organisations would you work with to promote her health, safety and well-being? Explain your reasons for suggesting these organisations.

Who can help Mrs Jones?

✿

✿

✿

✿

✿

Working with organisations

ACTIVITY

Talk to your manager about the benefits of working with other organisations in meeting the needs of the people you care for and support. Note down the three benefits that you think are most important and explain why you think they are important.

✿

✿

✿

Ways of working that can help improve partnership working

Partnership working in health and social care requires individuals from different organisations to work together with the people they care for and support to deliver a **holistic care package**. However, it is not always straightforward. Different organisations may have different budgets, workloads and service priorities, which individuals are not able to influence. Conflicts may arise if this is not recognised and taken into account. On a personal level, different people may have different ideas and approaches, which can be very helpful at times but, if not managed properly, can lead to disagreements.

key terms

Partnership working: this is when professionals from different departments or organisations come together to use their expertise to best help and support individuals.

Holistic care package: a combination of services put together to meet all of a person's needs.

Mr Ibrahim

CASE STUDY

Mr Ibrahim is having a few days in residential care after a long stay in hospital recovering from a broken hip and shoulder. The manager of the care home is required to put a care package together so that Mr Ibrahim can go home and remain as independent as possible. She has identified several different local health and social care organisations that could be brought together as a partnership to produce a care package to support Mr Ibrahim when he goes home. These include the following.

✿ Occupational therapy. This is an NHS service but it is hugely understaffed and cannot get out to assess Mr Ibrahim for at least a fortnight.

✿ Physiotherapy. This is also an NHS service but the physiotherapist and the care home manager disagree about Mr Ibrahim's physiotherapy needs.

✿ Support for you. This is an organisation that employs care workers to deliver personal care to people in their own homes. It has a reputation for employing staff who are not committed and are only in the job for the money.

✿ Movability. This is an organisation that provides and installs aids and adaptations for people who need help to live independently. The staff are very difficult to pin down and do not reply to voicemails and emails.

✿ Spick and Span. This is a new organisation that provides cleaning and laundry services. Their procedures are very rigid and the staff do not have any experience of working with people from different cultures.

Give three examples of conflicts within this partnership that you think might arise when they try to meet Mr Ibrahim's health and social care needs.

✿

✿

✿

Avoiding conflicts when working in partnership

To avoid conflicts when working in a partnership, you need to:

* communicate effectively and keep all partners informed about your work
* not let your opinions and beliefs get in the way of meeting health and social care needs; the partnership exists for the people who need care and support, not for you or your organisation
* know and understand everyone's role in the partnership, including your own
* show courtesy to, and respect for, everyone in the partnership, including the people who need care and support
* be flexible and prepared to learn new ways of doing things.

 ACTIVITY

Think about three meetings that you have recently attended. Use the table below to explain your contributions to making the meetings go well. An example has been done for you.

What I did to make the meeting go well	Why my behaviour helped the meeting go well
I listened to what everyone had to say and didn't interrupt.	It's polite to listen and not interrupt. Listening shows respect for the person who's speaking. It also shows that you're interested and want to understand what they have to say. If I don't listen, I won't get to know what everyone's roles are in giving care and support, including my own, which means I won't be able to fulfil my duty of care.

Skills and approaches for resolving conflicts

ACTIVITY

Think about a recent meeting with, for example, someone you care for and support, or with a group of colleagues that left you feeling frustrated and stressed.

1. What made you feel this way? Was there a clash of personalities or an argument, or did people behave inappropriately?

2. How do you think the meeting could have been run so that everyone would have come away feeling satisfied and in agreement about how to move forward?

There are countless ways of resolving conflicts but the main skills and approaches are to:

* find out exactly what caused the conflict and how people feel; stay calm, listen carefully and respect everyone's views
* explore different solutions; different people have different ideas about how to resolve a conflict
* try the agreed solution. If that doesn't work, try another.

ACTIVITY

Use an internet search engine to check for ways to resolve conflicts. Use what you find on the internet to create your own checklist below.

How and when to access support and advice

Your questions answered...

I've just moved to a hospital department where everyone seems to be in conflict. Every meeting I've attended so far has ended up with people quarrelling with each other for one reason or another. At this morning's **multidisciplinary meeting**, a colleague said I was 'not pulling my weight'. I was upset and embarrassed. I'm also angry because I really don't feel I was treated fairly. What should I do?

Everyone experiences problems from time to time in their partnership role and in coping with conflicts. Common problems include not being able to stay calm in tense situations, personality clashes, not being able to see things from someone else's point of view and being asked to do something that is outside the scope of your job role. Deal with the problem before it gets any worse by getting help as soon as you can. Sources of support and advice include the people you're conflicting with. Talk things through, tell them how you feel. You could also talk to a trusted colleague, your manager or a union representative. They'll give you honest, objective feedback and advice. Have a look at your workplace's procedures for dealing with conflicts. The last resort is to approach an organisation such as **ACAS**, which acts as a **neutral** third party in resolving conflicts.

key terms

Multidisciplinary meeting: this brings together people with different roles and specialities who have the same aims, for example to provide care and support.
ACAS: Advisory, Conciliation and Arbitration Service.
Neutral: unbiased, not taking sides.

ACTIVITY

Imagine that one of the people you care for and support has started objecting to the way you work with him, even though the procedures you are using have been agreed and are written into his care plan. He is angry and obstructive towards you. His parents are anxious as they want the best for their son. They want you to change the way you work, even though their suggestions would compromise their son's health and safety and you have not had the necessary training. At a team meeting, one of your colleagues has suggested that you 'Just do what the guy wants, anything to keep the peace.' You are worried and are starting to lose sleep over this issue.

1. Who can you go to for support and advice?

2. When should you get support and advice?

Assessor tip

Good sources of evidence of partnership working can arise from care planning and review meetings and from correspondence.

ACTIVITY

Keep a record of any problems you might have when working in partnerships and dealing with conflicts. Describe when and how you used support and advice to solve them. Ask a senior colleague to verify that you access support and advice in a timely manner by initialling each entry.

ARE YOU READY FOR ASSESSMENT?

☑ **Do you know the following:**

☐ 1. The difference between personal relationships and different types of working relationships?

☐ 2. The reasons for working to agreed ways of working and within the scope of your job role?

☐ 3. The importance of working in partnership with others?

☐ 4. The skills and approaches needed to resolve conflicts in partnerships?

☑ **Can you do the following:**

☐ 1. Access current information on agreed ways of working and implement them?

☐ 2. Work in ways that improve partnership working?

☐ 3. Access support and advice about partnership working and resolving conflicts?

UNIT HSC 036

Promote person-centred approaches in health and social care

This unit provides you with the knowledge and skills required to implement and promote person-centred care approaches. 'Person-centred' means that the emphasis is on helping the person as an individual to be as independent as possible, making decisions that are important to health and well-being and feeling empowered and in control.

A personalisation agenda is one in which individuals make decisions that affect their own lives but are supported by health care professionals.

You will need to be able to:
❁ understand the application of person-centred care approaches in health and social care
❁ work in a person-centred way
❁ establish consent when providing care or support
❁ implement and promote active participation
❁ support the individual's right to make choices
❁ promote the individual's well-being
❁ understand risk assessment in enabling a person-centred approach.

The application of person-centred care approaches

How person-centred values must influence all aspects of health and social care work

There has been a shift in recent years towards involving people more in their own care decisions. This affects the care and treatments they receive and gives them more ownership over how and when the plan of care is delivered. Person-centred values are the principles that underpin how individuals are treated when using person-centred approaches. The focus is on the individual to ensure they are at the centre of everything. When person-centred values and approaches are embedded into every aspect of care and support, people with disabilities are **empowered**, as they are equal partners in that care and support.

> **key term**
>
> **Empowered:** this is when an individual feels stronger, more confident or powerful owing to having more control over their life.

ACTIVITY

Complete the following table to provide a definition of some common person-centred values and an example of how you demonstrate these in practice.

Person-centred value	Definition	How I demonstrate this in my practice
Individuality.		
Rights.		
Choice.		
Independence.		
Privacy.		

Person-centred value	Definition	How I demonstrate this in my practice
Dignity.		
Partnership.		

key terms

Holistic health: a perspective that views the person as a whole, considering social, physical, intellectual, communication and emotional needs. General health and well-being are improved when all needs are met.

Person-centred care approach: this explores the likes, dislikes and preferences of each individual and ensures they have choice and control over their lives.

Open questions: these offer the opportunity to expand on the answer, for example by using 'How?', 'What?', 'Where?', 'When?' and give you more information, as opposed to closed questions that people can answer with just 'yes' or 'no'.

When you meet someone who will be entrusted to your care, you may be asked to collect information that will be recorded on a care plan. The type of information is linked to **holistic health**. This covers all the aspects of health in terms of how the individual manages the activities of daily living and maintains a sense of well-being. Applying a **person-centred care approach** means allowing for choices, control and individuality over these aspects.

Person-centred values and approaches are based on inclusion and the social model of disability. This model considers that it is the way society is organised that disables people and that helplessness is not an inevitable consequence of disability. An example of the impact of the social model of disability is the fact that all public buildings must be accessible to people with disabilities.

The social model differs from the medical model that was the dominant approach for many years. In the medical model, individuals and their abilities are defined by their medical condition, diagnosis or illness. This is based on the belief that individuals' medical needs were so serious that they could only ever be dependent on others to care for them. Professionals played a major role in decision making and, as a result, this further reduced individuals' independence. See SHC 33 'Promote equality and inclusion in health and social care settings', pages 60 and 62, for more information on the two models.

Holistic health and personalised care

ACTIVITY

Imagine you are interviewing someone who has been admitted to your residential care home.

1. Under the heading 'What I would need to know to deliver personalised care' enter two **open questions** that will give you an idea of that person's activities of daily living; their likes and dislikes, choices and preferences. An example has been done for you.

An activity of daily living	What I would need to know to deliver personalised care
Medication and health requirements.	How do you take your medications? How satisfied are you with your state of health and how your medications keep you well?
Goals for optimum well-being.	
Personal care routines, hygiene and dressing (any equipment needed).	
Managing mobility and any equipment and adaptations (shopping, household cleaning, cooking, laundry).	
Like to do and not like to do (preferences and dislikes over time and currently – involves a personal history).	
Socialisation – meeting people (visitors and going out).	
Food preferences, nutritional and hydration needs, leisure pursuits, culture and religious beliefs.	
Sleeping pattern.	

2. Summarise how you would find out this information if the person you were interviewing could not communicate with you.

Care plans in applying person-centred values

ACTIVITY

Read the cases of the two people below, including their care plans, which have been devised by the care team.

Below each section, explain what you think is wrong and what is missing. At the end, summarise the difference in approaches to explain why a person-centred plan would benefit the health and well-being of the two individuals. The first one has been done for you.

Mrs Robson

Mrs Robson is 82 years old and has diabetes, arthritis and a heart condition. She also has diverticulitis, which causes problems with her bowels from time to time. She was admitted to the home yesterday.

Medication: Give oral medication (as prescribed on the MAR) before breakfast at 7.30am. Would be useful to know how she feels this is benefitting her.

Physical and mobility needs: Able to walk short distances.

Diet: Normal diet but check blood sugar results.

Social and emotional: No problems, has settled well.

Hygiene: Give bowl in the mornings and can walk with frame to the toilet and manage shower.

Overall comment on the care plan:

Miss Nimak

Miss Nimak has been diagnosed with asthma and COPD (chronic obstructive pulmonary disease), which is making her increasingly breathless and tired, and unable to manage many physical tasks. The plan is to manage her care at home as she lives with her partner (who has a heart condition) and visits will be twice a day.

Medication: Inhalers and oral medication (as prescribed on the MAR). She can administer this herself.

Physical and mobility needs: Able to walk short distances but tires. One visit in the morning to assist with getting dressed and breakfast. Evening visit to ensure evening meal is taken and to help get ready for bed. Allow 15–20 minutes for visits.

Diet: Normal diet – give soft food if tiring quickly.

Social and emotional: Check on visits that previous depression is not apparent.

Hygiene: Manages to wash at the sink.

Overall comment on care plan:

ACTIVITY

Complete the following table by identifying at least two questions you could ask to evaluate how well person-centred values are embedded in the care planning. An example has been given for the first person-centred value.

Person-centred value	Questions to check how well the care plan demonstrates this value
Individuality.	1. Does the plan include the persons own words? 2.
Rights.	1. 2.
Choice.	1. 2.
Independence.	1. 2.
Privacy.	1. 2.
Dignity.	1. 2.
Respect.	1. 2.
Partnership.	1. 2.

Person-centred values should be in everyone's care plan

Assessor tip

Use this activity to evaluate a real care plan and discuss what you find with your assessor. Discuss what you could change to make the care plan more person-centred (if appropriate). This will provide good evidence of your knowledge and understanding.

A personalised and safe routine

Offering personalised care is essential to ensure you meet the needs of each individual in your care. You need to ensure that **personalisation** allows the best management for health, safety and holistic needs and fits in with the person's **best interests**.

All decisions made must be within your professional boundaries.

Work in a person-centred way

If you reflect on SHC 34 'Principles for implementing duty of care', you will remember the importance of having regard for each person's individuality, rights, choices, privacy, independence, dignity, respect and partnerships.

To remember these easily, take note of the acronym 'COPES' which is one way of ensuring that all aspects of daily living are being considered when planning care.

Choices. Having respect for the individual's own choice of clothes, personal routines, food preferences, leisure activities.

Ownership. The rights to privacy, dignity and measures for independence and **individuality**.

Partnerships. The services that are available to enable independence, health and welfare requirements.

Expression. Expressing opinions, views and feelings In terms of sustaining a personalised approach.

Spiritual. The likes, dislikes and preferences for enjoying a day to the full.

Personal history, preferences, wishes and needs

ACTIVITY

Look at the personal planning wheel on page 124.

Imagine you are being admitted to a care unit. Write your own wishes and daily routine in the appropriate sections in the wheel.

Think about what would be important to you if you were in a care home. How would you like your day to be filled? Would you like to be with others in a communal lounge or be on your own some of the time?

Think about your daily routine, what habits you might have and whether these can be accommodated. You may, for instance, like one hour of fresh air every day or always have a ginger biscuit with your tea! How would you manage this in partnership with others who care for you?

Imagine you normally collect a pension; who would do this for you and manage your financial affairs?

Compare these with a friend or colleague. How are they different?

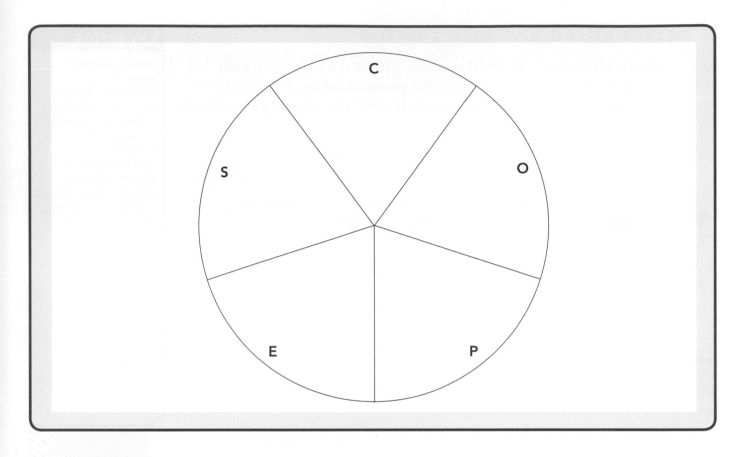

Marie

CASE STUDY

Marie is 42 years old and has profound learning disabilities following a brain injury four years previously. She now attends a day centre where the activities on offer are jigsaws, playing cards, painting and crafts.

Before her accident, Marie worked in a busy office as an administrative officer and was able to type quickly to prepare letters and documents. She is now unable to communicate well but can be understood if the care worker takes the time. Just recently she has been observed to be withdrawn or quite aggressive and irritable. One of the staff brought in a computer and Marie has begun to be engaged in typing again. Marie's mood has improved and her self-esteem seems to be higher.

Marie's mood has now improved

1. What aspects of the day centre are not person-centred?

2. What process does the case study omit for the consideration of person-centred care?

3. Why did the introduction of the computer appear to lift Marie's mood?

4. What further steps could be taken to build on this new enjoyment?

Other professionals

ACTIVITY

List at least four other health professionals or significant others who might be able to support the individuals who were described in the activity on pages 120–121.

✿ Mrs Robson is 82 years old and has diabetes, arthritis and a heart condition. She also has diverticulitis, which causes problems with her bowels from time to time. She was admitted to the home yesterday.

1.

2.

3.

4.

✿ Miss Nimak has been diagnosed with asthma and COPD (chronic obstructive pulmonary disease), which is making her increasingly breathless and tired, and unable to manage many physical tasks. The plan is to manage her care at home as she lives with her partner (who has a heart condition) and visits will be twice a day.

1.

2.

3.

4.

Putting person-centred values into practice, including complex or sensitive situations

Sometimes person-centred values will seem difficult to implement because of the complexity or the sensitivity of issues to consider. If the individual wants to pursue a behaviour that you think is not beneficial to health and well-being you must consider the benefits from the individual's point of view. Potential negative effects on health will need to be considered, discussed and reported. **Complex needs** involve consideration of more than one care aspect, such as heart failure, kidney failure, depression and perhaps breathing problems and obesity.

Complex or sensitive situations may include:
✿ death or bereavement of someone significant to the individual (including pets)
✿ breakdown of relationships
✿ traumatic situations, for example sudden death, an accident, sudden illness or an abusive/threatening incident
✿ instances when the individual's communication or cognitive needs are complex.

 **ACTIVITY**

Think about your work and the individuals you support. What situations do you consider to be complex and/or sensitive and why?

Adapting actions and approaches in response to an individual's changing needs

It is important to consider any **sensitive issues** in the event of a conflict of wishes for a care regime.

You will need to balance the care needs against the wishes of the person.

key terms

Complex needs: where there is a combination of factors that contribute to poor health and well-being.

Sensitive issue: an issue that raises potential disagreements with the accepted care regimes and means that risks may be taken to balance benefits for individuals.

ACTIVITY

Look at the following practice statements indicating 'rules' for effective support planning.

Some are accurate and some are not. Indicate whether you think the statement is true or false and give a reason for your decision. The first one has been done for you.

1. The person must complete the support plan on their own.
   False. The person is supported to make choices and decisions that will help and needs to consent to the plans.

2. Allow at least six hours of care time in every 24 hours.

3. Plan for contingencies and be flexible in case of changing needs.

4. The care factors discussed must fit in with the staff routine.

5. The people who make up the partnership are chosen by the individual.

6. Personal history is not part of the support plan.

7. The focus is on what is important **to** the individual.

8. Health and welfare needs must be considered under 'What is important **for** the individual'.

9. Other professionals are not allowed to join in with discussions owing to possible breaches of confidentiality.

10. Individual choices may involve sensitive decisions but these are not risk assessed for safety.

Your questions answered...

How often do I need to review a support plan for person-centred care?

This depends on the answers to 'Is everything working for you?', a question which appears in the care plan. It is very important to obtain consent for self-directed care plans; however, things change within someone's life and it is equally important to keep checking if person-centred care planning is working. This is based on the outcomes, that is, whether the person feels that they are living life independently and as fully as possible.

Establish consent when providing care or support

It is very important to establish consent from individuals when working in the health and social care sector because this is respecting the choices and wishes of the person.

Factors that influence the capacity of an individual to express consent

Information given should be clear and concise so that consent is given in an informed way. If individuals are unable to do this by writing things down, using sign language or verbally agreeing, there may be a need for an **advocate** to help.

Consent can be given in a written format, verbal format or implied, for example through a facial expression, nodding or reaching out for medication.

There are four types of consent.

✿ Informed consent – agreement that is based on full knowledge and understanding.

- Implied consent – when the person's actions give the impression they are consenting, for example attending the Accident and Emergency department of a hospital for treatment.
- Continued consent – where consent continues during the course of treatment, care or support.
- Consent by proxy – if the person is unable to give consent, decisions are made by an appropriate person, for example their next of kin or an advocate.

Establish consent for an activity or action

It is important when seeking an individual's consent that you also establish their capacity (ability) to consent. The capacity to consent means the individual is able to:

- fully understand the information that relates to the decision to be made
- retain that information long enough to make a decision
- make sense of the information and reach a decision, that is, understand the positives and negatives
- express their decision to others.

The capacity to consent can change as a result of the individual's medical condition and this also needs to be considered. For example, an individual with dementia may have changing cognitive ability because of the type of dementia they have.

ACTIVITY

Suggest the following actions you would take when establishing consent for individuals with the following conditions. The consent could be for administering a new medication, a procedure or implementing a new activity or action.

Condition	Procedure for establishing consent
Unable to sign for consent.	
Unable to speak.	

Condition	Procedure for establishing consent
Complex needs prevent any consent being established by that individual.	

Steps to take if consent cannot be readily established

ACTIVITY

Complete the gaps in the following sentences using the words below.

reassurance   methods   advocates   Mental Capacity Act   judgements
aware   contingencies   difficult   decisions   establish

* It is important for a carer or support worker to _____ the factors that might affect the ability to consent.

* If the person cannot verbally communicate, or finds it difficult to do so, ways must be sought to support the choices of that person and _____ recorded.

* Under the _____ _____ _____, other representatives or _____ can make _____ on their behalf.

* If steps taken to establish consent are proving _____, professionals who can provide supporting _____ must be contacted.

* If services are not be available, the person must be made _____ of this and _____ given that _____ will be sought.

Assessor tip

Remember that you will need to show your assessor how you establish consent each time you support individuals. You do this by explaining what you plan to do and checking that the individual is still happy to continue.

130

Implement and promote active participation

It is important to recognise that a person has the right to live as independently as possible and be an active partner in their care regime rather than being a **passive recipient**. They know best what they want, and if their wishes are met, within the boundaries of what is possible, their well-being will improve.

Different ways of applying active participation

If you plan care in partnership with the individual and others, you are encouraging **active participation** of the individual. The individual's physical and mental abilities will need to be considered and the amount of assistance required may be small or large, depending on assessments and joint decisions.

It is important to discuss the individual's perceived needs and agree the level of help required and when it will be needed. Applying active participation means organising support around the individual, not fitting them into existing services. This approach will build the individual's self-confidence and self-esteem and will empower them as they will feel listened to, and valued, as an equal partner. The focus on their goals and wishes means they have a vested interest in success and are more likely to engage in activities and work to overcome barriers.

Agree how active participation will be implemented

> **key terms**
>
> **Passive recipient:** the person is subject to others' ideas of what will benefit them rather than being consulted.
>
> **Active participation:** this is when individuals are fully involved in all aspects of care and treatments, taking part in activities that they wish to, and agreeing activities in partnership with others.

ACTIVITY

Read the statements in the first column of the table below. You may hear some of them in your workplace.

Decide whether you agree with the statement or not. Then write your comments about promoting a person-centred approach and active participation. An example has been done for you.

Statement	Agree or disagree?	Ways to promote person-centred care and active participation
Medication should only be administered by a trained professional.	Disagree.	If a risk assessment has been carried out, then a person can be deemed as safe to give their own medication even if this involves CDs (controlled drugs). Information, such as any side effects and effects of non-compliance, will need to be explained before the person gives consent.
People with dementia are unable to do anything for themselves.		

Statement	Agree or disagree?	Ways to promote person-centred care and active participation
Legally, an employer has to make their premises wheelchair-friendly.		
A person who is consulted and included in the management of their health needs will have better self-esteem.		
Person-centred care means the person has to be seen to be treated.		

How active participation can address the holistic needs

Often, if one need is met then others are too. For example, if you accompany an individual on a shopping trip, you are promoting physical needs (mobility) but also their general health and well-being, and their emotional, social and communication needs.

Promote understanding and use of active participation

ACTIVITY

Read the following snapshots of individuals.

Use the space provided to identify how you might support the holistic needs (physical, social, emotional, communication, health and well-being) of each individual and allow for active participation.

1. Brian says that he never has a bath as this means washing in dirty water. The home where he has been transferred to is in need of modernisation and has only one shower. He never eats pork and likes to eat alone in his room, not in the communal room.

2. Marianne has severe sight loss but can manage meals and hygiene. She has been given a white cane so she can go out. She is afraid to do this and fears her shopping trips may have ended.

3. Riley is an independent 82-year-old man who has been admitted to a small residential home managed by a warden because he was not coping with independent living. He used to love to drink beer in the evenings and at Sunday lunchtime. His new residence is a short walk from a pub.

Support the individual's right to make choices

You cannot make a choice regarding a care strategy unless you know the range of choices that are available to you.

Support an individual to make informed choices

You need to have an understanding of what is happening in an individual's life in order to adapt care and support choices with options. For example, do they have the relevant information or any ideas about how they can adapt and improve their lifestyle? Understanding the implications of each available option – both the benefits and the potential negatives – is also an important part of making an informed choice. It is important that information is presented in an objective way and the individual is given time to ask questions and consider the options before making a decision. Some people may prefer to have information in written form, as they may understand it better if they are able to read it several times.

Assessor tip

Your assessor could observe you undertaking a care plan review for a service user for whom you have key worker responsibility. This will provide good quality evidence of how you have promoted active participation.

Use own role and authority to support the individual's right to make choices

ACTIVITY

You have started work in a community setting that has been short staffed for some time, with different carers visiting the following residents. You notice the following comments made in recent reports about three people that you visit. Explain your response to each person, in order to give information and choices to improve the health need identified. An example has been done for you.

Person with health need identified in report	Information and choices that you might give
Mrs A is not eating or drinking well and is becoming dehydrated and confused.	Mrs A needs information about her condition deteriorating because of not being well hydrated or eating properly. She needs nutritional advice, encouragement to drink plenty and to check who is helping her to prepare and cook meals. There may be a need for a meals service. Mrs A needs to be aware that poor nutrition and not drinking will cause confusion and possibly headaches and problems with her kidneys.
Mrs B has been crying a lot recently, possibly because of social isolation and depression.	
Mr C, aged 88, has been told he can no longer drive because of his poor eyesight. He loves the freedom his car gives him and his disabled wife.	

Manage risk in a way that maintains the individual's right to make choices

The risk assessment process needs to ensure that it enables people to do what they want to do without being harmed.

ACTIVITY

Read the choices below and indicate at least two risk factors that need to be assessed.

Individual choices	Risk factors
Mrs D wants to self-medicate and look after her own pain relief.	

Individual choices	Risk factors
Mr E, with poor eyesight, wants to make his own meals.	
Mrs F wants to live in her own home but has an open fire and her mental health has deteriorated with increased confusion.	

Support an individual to question or challenge decisions

 ACTIVITY

Imagine the people in the previous activity have received negative feedback from their carers. When they asked about being able to look after themselves, they were told 'You are not safe to do this.'

Describe what steps and processes will support them to question or challenge decisions impacting on their independence.

Issues and decisions	How will you support them to challenge this decision?
Mrs D wants to self-medicate and look after her own pain relief but has been told there are too many complications.	
Mr E, with poor eyesight, wants to make his own meals but has been told he may burn himself.	
Mrs F wants to live in her own home but has an open fire and her mental health has deteriorated with increased confusion. She has been told the house is unsafe for her to stay in over the winter.	

Awareness of assisted technology and resources

The following activity helps you to understand how other professionals and assisted technology or resources may help people with specific needs. Maintaining awareness of what services or equipment are accessible makes your job more rewarding as it can help individuals to gain a better quality of life.

ACTIVITY

Research the technology or services that can be provided for individuals with the following disabilities. For each, give one service and one piece of equipment.

1. A person with a hearing impairment who is embarrassed in the company of large groups.

2. A person who is registered blind and is no longer able to enjoy reading books.

3. A person with COPD (chronic obstructive pulmonary disease) and shortness of breath who wants to carry on working.

4. A wheelchair user who has a passion for gardening and the outdoors but has steps to her house.

Assessor tip

Use a risk assessment you have completed as a basis for a discussion with your assessor.

Promote the individual's well-being

If you reflect back on the first two activities on pages 117 and 119, you will remember that well-being can only be achieved if the holistic care needs are fully met. Check your understanding of physical, social and emotional needs, health needs and communication and intellectual needs.

The links between identity, self-image and self-esteem

Everyone has their own **identity**, a combination of appearance, culture, background, characteristics and traits.

This links with **self-image**, which is how you perceive yourself. This may be positive or negative.

If you dislike your identity and have negative perceptions of how you look and behave, then your **self-esteem** will be low.

Self-esteem develops through our comparison of ourselves with others. If a person compares themselves positively to others and considers themselves to be as able, attractive and as good as others, they can be said to have a high self-esteem. Individuals who consider themselves to be less attractive, less able and inferior to others have a low self-esteem. Our self-esteem impacts on how we respond to other people.

Our self-image combines with self-esteem to form our identity. It develops through our relationships and interactions with others and this helps us to become aware of our physical, emotional, intellectual and social abilities, attributes and qualities.

The factors that contribute to the well-being of individuals

When we think about well-being, we are thinking in terms of how we feel we are doing and whether our life is enjoyable and fulfilling. Well-being is usually related to:

* our values and attitudes, for example hopes, fears, self-esteem, moral codes, having meaning in our life
* practical aspects of our life, for example work, income, education, physical and mental health
* our personal and social relationships, for example family, friends, intimate relationships.

For some people, well-being means feeling valued by others and having a purpose and meaning in their life. For others, well-being is closely linked to the absence of physical or mental illness. Everyone uses different measures to determine their state of well-being.

key terms

Identity: the characteristics that make you who you are.

Self-image: how you perceive yourself – your impression of who you are.

Self-esteem: a way of feeling about oneself that can be positive or negative depending on how a person perceives their identity and self-image. Low self-esteem can potentially affect health and well-being.

ACTIVITY

Explain why you think the following people have a low self-esteem by describing the link between their identity and self-image. Indicate the holistic factors that will suffer as time goes on.

1. Miss G has been trying to lose weight unsuccessfully and now refuses to go out with friends or socialise.

2. Mr H loved his job as a long-distance lorry driver and was always a very cheerful man. A severe leg injury caused him to lose his right leg, which ended his driving career. His wife says he is now very quiet.

3. Mrs I has had depression for years and fears being in crowded places or at events where she has to meet people.

Support an individual in a way that promotes their sense of identity, self-image and self-esteem

ACTIVITY

Describe how you might support each of the individuals in the previous activity.

1. Miss G has been trying to lose weight unsuccessfully and now refuses to go out with friends or socialise.

2. Mr H loved his job as a long-distance lorry driver and was always a very cheerful man. A severe leg injury caused him to lose his right leg, which ended his driving career. His wife says he is now very quiet.

3. Mrs I has had depression for years and fears being in crowded places or at events where she has to meet people.

Contribute to an environment that promotes well-being

Analysing the factors that make up holistic needs and self esteem will help you to support people in very clear ways. By ensuring that the environment is supporting and encouraging, and where the person is actively participating in their own care, you will be demonstrating that you contribute to the general health and well-being of people.

 ACTIVITY

Categorise the following abilities and activities of daily living by ticking the appropriate columns.

Physical: P   Social: S   Emotional: E
Health: H   Communication: C   Intellectual: I

Be aware that more than one category may apply to an activity, so there may be more than one tick across the chart.

Abilities/Activities	P	S	E	H	C	I
Being able to wash and dress oneself.						
Being able to pay own bills.						
Being able to meet with friends for coffee.						

Abilities/Activities	P	S	E	H	C	I
To learn more about taking good photos and attend a college.						
To manage own cooking and household chores.						
To go for a walk, swim, keep fit, fishing or play golf.						
To manage own toilet needs and get in and out of bed.						
Being able to watch and listen to the TV, music and the radio, and being able to make a telephone call.						
Being able to read and write.						
Being able to manage medications or special diets.						

Assessor tip

Treating people with dignity, respect and in ways that affirm their value and identity demonstrates how you promote their well-being, so remember this in every interaction.

key term

Self-directed support: working in partnership with health professionals to manage self-care with identified support strategies.

Risk assessment in enabling a person-centred approach

There are sometimes activities that we want to allow the person to manage in accordance with their wishes and **self-directed support** but that do not pass the test of being completely risk free. Risk assessment is not only required by law it is also part of responsible practice, so we should take steps to show we have considered potential risks and have taken steps to reduce the possibility of negative effects on people being supported. Risk assessment needs to be objective and focused on enabling the individual to undertake an activity as safely as possible. Involving others in the risk assessment process will increase the commitment to enabling the individual while minimising the risks involved. It is also important for everyone to understand the measures in place that manage and minimise any identified risks and maintain a consistent approach in applying agreed management strategies. In practice, this means using and applying risk assessment tools consistently and according to agreed procedures.

Risk assessing practice

Risk assessment consists of five steps.

1. Identify the hazards and associated risks.

2. Decide who might be harmed and how.

3. Evaluate the risks to determine what will reduce them.

4. Record the findings.

5. Monitor, review and revise.

Compare different uses of risk assessment in health and social care

ACTIVITY

Describe an **environmental** and a **personal** factor for risk assessing in the following circumstances. An example has been done for you.

	Infection control risks when serving food	A person self-medicating with controlled drugs	A wheelchair user living alone
Environmental.	Is the hygiene of a good standard in the kitchen and the eating area (tables, utensils and crockery)?		
Personal.			

How risk-taking and risk assessment relate to rights and responsibilities

There are some sensitive issues that you will need to take more time to consider. Never rush complex or sensitive issues when the objective is to enable people to exercise their rights and choices. The next activity is an example of a sensitive situation to be risk assessed.

Why risk assessments need to be regularly revised

ACTIVITY

Marlon, aged 20, lives with his older brother Jacob, who is a known drug user. You are working as a community care assistant and your manager wants your opinion regarding Marlon's safety at home. The local college where Marlon is a student contacted Social Services because he turned up one day having 'smoked something'. Marlon says this was not true.

You now meet with him for the first time.

1. The following actions may occur in the meeting but are in the wrong order. You need to rearrange the order of the actions to give the meeting a purposeful structure. Then you need to identify which of the five risk assessment steps applies to each action. Remember, there might be more than one step that matches each action. Complete the table below with the correct structure of the meeting and the risk assessment step (see page 140) that the action complies with. The first two have been done for you.

   ✿ Suggest support networks and regular contact in the future.

   ✿ Write notes and highlight the risk assessment steps to minimise risks, review the plan and gain consent.

   ✿ Introduce yourself and explain your interest in his welfare.

   ✿ Give Marlon your contact telephone number and email address to maintain a progress report.

   ✿ Offer alternatives to living with Jacob.

   ✿ Ask him how he can ensure his own safety while living with Jacob.

   ✿ Establish his interests, views on college, sport, hobbies, music and friends.

   ✿ Reflect and verbally summarise his self-esteem, confidence, ability to be independent and wishes.

   ✿ Agree an action plan to review before leaving.

   ✿ Pass on your findings to your line manager and plan dates for review.

Meeting structure	Risk assessment steps
Introduce yourself and explain your interest in his welfare.	N/A
Establish his interests, views on college, sport, hobbies, music and friends.	Step 1

Meeting structure	Risk assessment steps

2. Describe why this kind of situation will need to be regularly reviewed.

Mrs Turench

 CASE STUDY

Mrs Turench is an 84-year-old Turkish-Cypriot woman who has arrived on the unit where you work. You are told she has suffered chest pains but she is being admitted for respite care. She has arrived half an hour before you are due to leave for the day. The unit is very busy and you cannot get any immediate help.

You try to ask her about her holistic needs and, by using basic English and signing, she manages to let you know some information about herself. Periodically she breaks into Turkish and looks out of the window, trying the window handles as if wanting to get out.

The scene

'Here very bad' (pointing to chest, panting and indicating shortness of breath).

'See' (points to fingers and hip joints indicating pain).

Shakes head a lot, appearing confused and perplexed, saying repeatedly, 'What I will do? What I will do?'

You note she is unsteady on her feet and has a walking stick but is examining the window and trying to open it in exasperation.

She shows you all her tablets but then shrugs her shoulders and goes back to the window.

A new arrival on the unit

1. What are the risk factors for Mrs Turench's health and safety needs?

2. What are your concerns regarding the holistic health needs of Mrs Turench?

3. What information do you still need in terms of person-centred care, and who do you think needs contacting?

4. What must you ensure is reported to your manager before you go off duty?

5. Describe what risk factors will need revisiting, why and when.

ARE YOU READY FOR ASSESSMENT?

☑ **Do you know the following:**

☐ **1.** How and why person-centred values must influence all aspects of health and social care work?

☐ **2.** How to evaluate the use of care plans in applying person-centred values?

☐ **3.** How to analyse factors that influence the capacity of an individual to express consent?

☐ **4.** The steps to take if consent cannot be readily established?

☐ **5.** Different ways to apply active participation to meet an individual's holistic needs?

☐ **6.** How to support individuals to question or challenge decisions concerning them that are made by others?

☐ **7.** How identity and self-esteem are linked to well-being?

☐ **8.** How to analyse factors that contribute to an individual's well-being?

☐ **9.** Compare different uses of risk assessment in health and social care?

☐ **10.** How risk-taking and risk assessment relate to rights and responsibilities?

☐ **11.** Why risk assessments need to be regularly reviewed?

☑ **Can you do the following:**

☐ 1. Work in a person-centred way that takes into account an individual's history, preferences, wishes and needs?

☐ 2. Use person-centred values in complex and sensitive situations?

☐ 3. Adapt actions and approaches in response to an individual's changing needs or preferences?

☐ 4. Establish consent when providing care and support?

☐ 5. Work with individuals and others to agree how to implement active participation?

☐ 6. Show how active participation can address an individual's holistic needs?

☐ 7. Promote understanding and use of active participation?

☐ 8. Support individuals to make informed choices?

☐ 9. Use your role and authority to support individual choices?

☐ 10. Manage risk in ways that maintain individuals' rights to make choices?

☐ 11. Support individuals in ways that promote their sense of identity, self-image and self-esteem?

☐ 12. Contribute to an environment that promotes well-being?

UNIT HSC 037

Promote and implement health and safety in health and social care

This unit will help you to understand your role and responsibilities, and those of others, in promoting and maintaining a safe, healthy environment within a health and social care setting.

Activities will support your knowledge, awareness and skill gathering to help you to continuously monitor health and safety as you work with colleagues and individuals in your care. You must work within a legal framework and this unit will also help you to see how this informs the procedures you follow and your general day-to-day practice.

You will need to be able to:

- ✿ understand own responsibilities and responsibilities of others relating to health and safety
- ✿ carry out own responsibilities for health and safety
- ✿ understand procedures for responding to accidents and sudden illness
- ✿ reduce the spread of infection
- ✿ move and handle equipment and other objects safely
- ✿ handle hazardous substances and materials
- ✿ promote fire safety in the work setting
- ✿ implement security measures in the work setting
- ✿ know how to manage stress.

Responsibilities and those of others relating to health and safety

Some hazards in the work setting may be obvious to you, such as a spillage or an obstruction to a doorway. You will ensure that the spillage is mopped up or the obstruction is removed and then carry on with your duties.

Other incidents may be potentially serious and you will need to consider reporting these to your manager.

You are required to work within a legal framework that will inform settings of the different policies and procedures to follow. It is important to remember to work within your job role. If you are unsure of the boundaries regarding your job role, then seek advice from your manager. Organisational policies and procedures will also guide you about your responsibilities, both legal and as an employee, as these will be based on health and safety legislation requirements. The first activity will test your knowledge of the legislation in place that comes under the Health and Safety at Work Act 1974. Many Acts and codes of practice have been derived from this over the years, but you need to be aware of legislation relating to health and safety in a health and social care setting.

Identify health and safety legislation in a health and social care setting

ACTIVITY

Your duties are listed in the left-hand column. Legislation and guidance is listed in the right-hand column. Draw lines to match up the correct legislation that governs the task you perform. Some duties may come under more than one piece of legislation or guidance.

You may need to research the full meaning of COSHH and RIDDOR.

Duties

1. Reading the manufacturer's instructions before diluting cleaning fluid.
2. Making a report after a visitor has a nasty fall in the care home.
3. Checking that the hoist is in good working order before lifting a resident.
4. Placing clinical waste in a yellow bag and labelling it with its contents and location for incineration.
5. Checking that fire doors are kept closed and free from obstruction.
6. Conducting a risk assessment for lone working.
7. Using a probe to check the core temperature of a cooked chicken.
8. Wearing disposable gloves when giving a bed pan.
9. Checking the contents of the first aid box.

Legislation or guidance

A. Infection Control Guidelines (Department of Health)

B. Food Safety Act 1990

C. Manual Handling Operations 1992

D. RIDDOR 1995

E. COSHH 2002

F. Management of Health and Safety 1999

G. Regulations Reform (Fire Safety) Order 2005

H. Health and Safety (First Aid) Regulations 1981

The main points of policies and procedures as they apply to you

ACTIVITY

The pictures below relate to duties that you may perform. For each picture, devise a step-by-step procedure that may help a new member of staff. Each procedure should use the key words given to create the four or five important steps of good practice that ensure you comply with agreed ways of working (policies and procedures). Explain the reason for your decisions. The first one has been done for you.

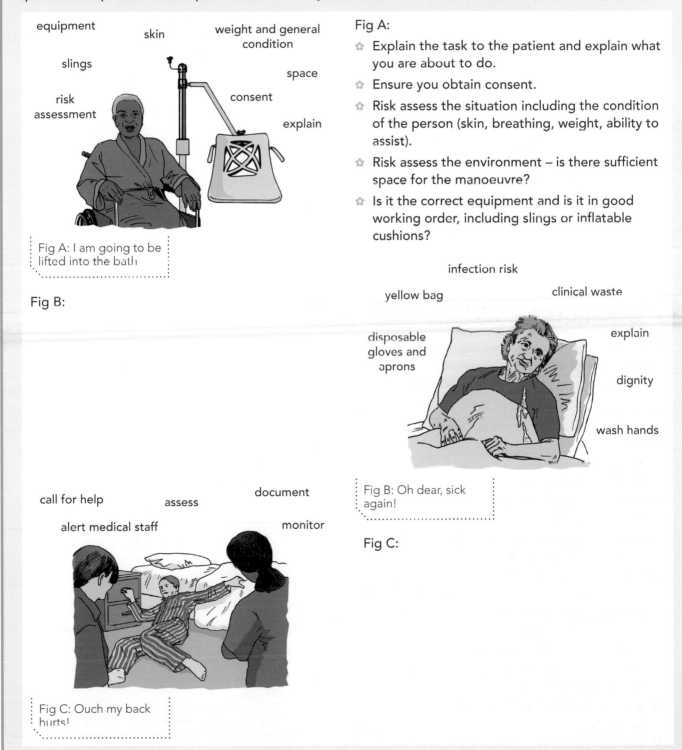

equipment

skin

weight and general condition

slings

space

risk assessment

consent

explain

Fig A: I am going to be lifted into the bath

Fig A:

✿ Explain the task to the patient and explain what you are about to do.

✿ Ensure you obtain consent.

✿ Risk assess the situation including the condition of the person (skin, breathing, weight, ability to assist).

✿ Risk assess the environment – is there sufficient space for the manoeuvre?

✿ Is it the correct equipment and is it in good working order, including slings or inflatable cushions?

Fig B:

infection risk

yellow bag

clinical waste

disposable gloves and aprons

explain

dignity

wash hands

Fig B: Oh dear, sick again!

Fig C:

call for help

assess

document

alert medical staff

monitor

Fig C: Ouch my back hurts!

Carry out own responsibilities for health and safety

Policies and procedures or other agreed ways of working

A key element of the Health and Safety Commission's 'Strategy for Workplace Health and Safety in Britain to 2010 and beyond' required all staff to be involved in promoting and maintaining health, safety and security. Risk assessments are a means by which you aim to identify hazards and the potential risks they represent. Once identified, measures can be put in place to remove the hazard or minimise the risk of harm that it represents.

It is important that you revisit the five steps of risk assessing (see page 140) because this is essential in nearly every duty you perform. It is also a legal requirement.

Risk assessment and ways to minimise potential risks and hazards

Think about what risks need to be assessed in the next case study.

Alice

CASE STUDY

Alice is 88 and lives on the ground floor of a residential home. She is mobile with a stick but unsteady on her feet because of impaired vision. She also has impaired hearing. She likes to take a shower, dress herself and go for morning coffee in the lounge. She relies on furniture being in the same place and has had a fall because someone recently moved a chair.

She is not too well this morning, being more unsteady on her feet than usual, and would like someone to help her.

1. What are the possible **risks** that you may encounter during this personal care routine?

2. What will you need to do before preparing to help Alice and what are the possible options?

3. What resources or equipment might you use and why?

4. What might be a possible **hazard**?

5. How do you monitor a safe environment for those with poor mobility or vision?

6. Reflect back and describe the five steps to risk assessing in terms of helping Alice.

Analyse your own responsibilities for health and safety

You are accountable in the workplace for maintaining the agreed ways of working to promote and maintain health and safety. This includes being competent and confident in the procedures you carry out during every shift. It also includes the responsibility to keep yourself healthy, as you are in regular contact with service users, patients and colleagues. The issues below will be explored in more detail later in this unit, but it is good to test yourself on the reasons for the procedures in your workplace. Many of these relate to being safe and sensible or avoiding cross-contamination (see 'Reduce the spread of infection' on page 159).

The next activity helps you to think about policy statements and agreed ways of working.

key terms

Risks: the possibility of suffering harm or being exposed to danger.
Hazard: the presence of anything that can cause actual harm.

Support others to understand and follow safe practices

ACTIVITY

Read the following statements and place a tick if you think it is true. In the second column give your reasons as to why you think they are true or false, as if you were explaining them to new recruits

Statements	Reason
Work clothing should not be worn outside the work environment.	
Jewellery carries bacteria and so should not be worn.	
You do not need to wash hands prior to wearing disposable gloves or when using alcohol gel.	
Updating training on first aid, food hygiene and manual handling is essential.	
PPE (personal and protective equipment) does not include shoes.	
Risk assessing activities is a legal requirement.	
You do not need to report a security incident.	
You must lift manually if equipment is being used by someone else.	
You can administer medicines once you know the names of residents.	
Sharps boxes should not be more than two-thirds full when you dispose of them.	

Access additional support or information relating to health and safety

Managers, deputy managers and team leaders have a responsibility to manage others and ensure they follow guidelines and procedures in line with legislation. This next activity will help you to understand their roles and responsibilities, which might one day be yours, if you become a manager. Research anything you are not sure about and add your source at the bottom of the table.

Employer's responsibilities: monitor and report potential health and safety risks

  **ACTIVITY**

Read the following statements regarding your employer or manager's role in promoting health and safety. Place a tick by the statement if you think it is true, give your reasons in the second column.

Statements	Reason
An employer provides information about risks to health and safety.	
An employer has a responsibility to provide you with the appropriate training in order to do your job.	
There will be policies on sickness and absence that you will need to sign.	
Fire safety procedures are an optional training opportunity.	
Equality and diversity policy means that there are no dress codes in health and social care settings.	
An employer will arrange for an induction into health and safety procedures.	

Statements	Reason
It is the duty of an employer or manager to assess a worker as being competent when handling medicines or performing specialised duties such as administering oxygen.	
An employer should make visitors aware of health and safety requirements.	
There has to be five employees or more in order to have written policies in place.	
The employer or manager is not responsible for staff shortages on night duties when the manager has gone home.	

Special training

ACTIVITY

Some duties or tasks, whether you perform them regularly or not, cannot be done without special training. If you perform a duty you have not been trained to do, you will have to take the consequences for any errors made.

Look at the tasks below and identify the special training you would need in order to do this task. Indicate if you think you need to be observed to be competent before doing this without supervision, then describe a possible error that could occur if you had no training for this task. An example has been done for you.

Tasks	Type of training needed	Do I need to be observed?	Possible errors without training
Administering a subcutaneous injection.	'Safe Handling of Medicines' or similar accredited programme.	Yes.	Errors may be the incorrect administering of the injection (and wrong drug), which could cause serious harm to the person.
Giving someone CPR (cardio-pulmonary resuscitation).			

Tasks	Type of training needed	Do I need to be observed?	Possible errors without training
Using a hoist to lift a heavy woman into a bath.			
Inserting a pessary.			
Administering oxygen via a face mask using.			
Cooking sausages for 20 people.			
Changing a dressing using an aseptic technique.			
Transferring a patient from bed to chair using a board.			

What can I do if we are short staffed and I am asked to do a task that I have observed only once?

You must inform your line manager that you are not yet competent to do this. It is very important that you should never do anything that you feel uncomfortable about or have not been trained to do. Remember that you are accountable for your actions. So, performing a duty when you are unsure about the risks involved, or the procedures, may cause harm to the individual.

Monitor and report potential health and safety risks

It is part of your duty of care and the code of practice to monitor and report risks, potential hazards and actual accidents to your manager. Reporting of incidents, accidents, dangerous diseases and occurrences forms the legal requirement of RIDDOR.

Potential hazards, if spotted as part of a daily risk assessment process, can help to prevent a serious accident or incident from occurring. It is recommended practice now for organisations to appoint a **health and safety representative**.

Awareness of potential hazards

 ACTIVITY

Imagine that you have been appointed as the health and safety representative in your workplace.

1. Circle the hazards that you notice in the lounge.

2. Identify the hazards that you should report to your manager.

3. Research the duties and role of a health and safety representative by visiting the website of the HSE (Health and Safety Executive) at www.hse.org.uk.

Procedures for responding to accidents and sudden illness

The Health and Safety (First Aid) Regulations 1981 require employers to provide appropriate equipment, facilities and personnel qualified to deliver first aid treatments in the workplace.

It is the responsibility of the setting to risk assess the workforce, the number of residents or patients and the duties performed, to estimate how many staff should be qualified first aiders.

Different types of accidents and sudden illnesses that may occur

 ACTIVITY

Read the following accidents or sudden signs of illness and describe your **immediate** actions. You should aim for at least three actions.

You may need to check these using the internet or other sources if you have not completed a first aid course. Do not worry about giving a lot of detail regarding first aid measures, but there are basic procedures that you should follow in order to ensure people's safety, even if you have not been trained. Ask your manager if you could attend an approved training course.

1. Mr Salmon has sustained a cut finger and it is bleeding quite profusely.

2. Mrs O'Brien, who is a diabetic, has been vomiting but now she appears confused, drowsy and disorientated.

3. Mr Trigg is making gasping noises and appears to be choking.

4. Mrs Lantern has fallen down three steps outside and has banged her head on a wall.

5. Amina is discovered unconscious on the floor.

6. Mrs Hussain has a severe nose bleed.

7. Barbara, the cleaner, is having difficulty breathing and you notice extreme puffiness and swelling of her face and neck. You know she is allergic to certain substances.

8. Su-Yin has collapsed and is not breathing.

Procedures after an incident or accident

It is important for you to understand the legal requirements of reporting any accident, incident or death that happens on site. Try to look at an example of an accident report form from your workplace or download one from the HSE website (www.hse.gov.uk).

You must be able to pass on the details of any accident or incident to your manager, employer or medical personnel, so be as observant as you can and inform them of any known medical history. Relatives must also be informed, the incident investigated, the first aid box refilled and any blood and body fluids disposed of in accordance with procedures.

Reduce the spread of infection

Controlling the spread of potential infections is everyone's responsibility – whether they are a team member or a visitor.

Supporting others to follow practices that reduce the spread of infection

If you have an understanding of how infections can spread, you can support others to follow good practice.

Remember, bacteria are everywhere and actually help to protect us from illness through our immune system. **Pathogenic bacteria**, however, can make us ill, particularly if we belong to a **vulnerable group**.

Bacteria grow when certain conditions are present, such as warmth, moisture, a food source, time to multiply and air. **Cross-contamination** occurs when large numbers of bacteria have been transferred from one object or source to another. These include from a person, sheets, handkerchiefs, drinking glasses, water, food, blood and so on.

Reducing the possibility of infections means that you have to break the cycle or route of transmission. There are different ways that microorganisms can spread, and understanding about these will help you to prevent infections.

- Droplets or airborne infections: examples are coughing and sneezing.
- Direct contact with another person: examples are touching, holding hands or sexual contact with an infected person.
- Indirect contact: examples are infected items, such as dirty handkerchiefs or sputum containers.
- Ingested: for example, eating contaminated food.
- Via the bloodstream: for example, infected needles or bites and stings that enter via breaks in the skin or mucous membranes.

key terms

Pathogenic bacteria: bacteria that are harmful and can make us ill.

Vulnerable group: babies, young children, older people and adults with weak immune systems are more susceptible to disease and illness caused by pathogenic bacteria.

Cross-contamination: this is when a contaminated source or object has come into contact with another source, for example when unwashed hands touch vulnerable service users.

Routes of transmission

ACTIVITY

Complete the gaps in the following sentences using the terms below.

hygiene   airborne   contaminated   contact   host   toilet
blood   digestive   soiled   clinical   smaller   fluids   viruses
aprons   air   time   hand washing   gloves

* Bacteria can circulate in the air; this is known as _____. They can also be spread via _____ and body _____ and through the _____ system, for instance when eating _____ food.

* _____ are also pathogenic and easily spread by direct _____ with other people.

* They are _____ than bacteria and do not need the five growth factors of warmth, _____ moisture, food and _____.

* They just need a living _____ cell.

* The most important thing we can do to prevent infection in care environments is to maintain good _____.

* This involves frequent _____ _____ in between caring for individuals, before handling _____ linen and medicines and after using the _____.

* Disposable _____ and _____ should be worn when dealing with _____ waste.

See www.dh.gov.uk.

Assessor tip

Demonstrating your competence is not limited to your assessor observing your hand washing technique when working directly with service users; it includes all infection control measures. Therefore, remember to ensure your assessor and other visitors comply with infection control measures, for example by using hand gel upon arrival.

The recommended method for hand washing

It is not good enough just to run your hands quickly under cool water when washing your hands. You must get into a habit of washing your hands thoroughly by following published guidelines. We all carry organisms on our hands, and about 40 per cent of us are natural carriers of the pathogenic organism *Methicillin-resistant Staphylococcus aureus*, more commonly known as MRSA, which can be very dangerous to vulnerable people in hospitals and nursing homes. These bacteria live on skin and present a risk when vulnerable people have open wounds. When caring for others, it is crucial to wash your hands frequently. If this is difficult then you should use an alcohol gel. The gel, however, is no substitute for effective hand washing with liquid soap and warm water.

See www.dh.gov.uk.

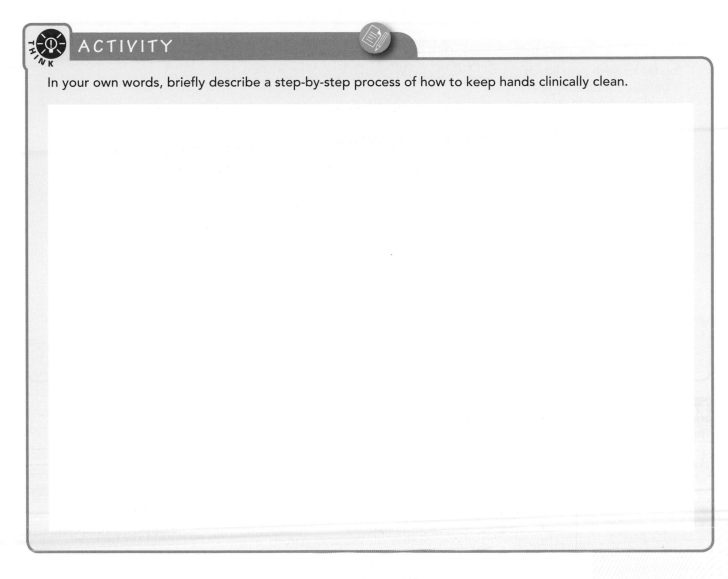

ACTIVITY

In your own words, briefly describe a step-by-step process of how to keep hands clinically clean.

Ensure that your own health and hygiene does not pose a risk to others

An important part of the agreed way of working is to keep yourself healthy. If you think you are a risk to others (perhaps because you are unwell), whether these are individuals in your care, visitors or colleagues, you must not come to the workplace.

ACTIVITY

Describe how your own state of health and poor hygiene practices may harm others in the following circumstances.

Circumstance	Risks to others
You have just returned from holiday; you are due back at work but you have gastroenteritis.	

Circumstance	Risks to others
You fail to wash your hands in between supporting each individual who is in your care.	
You have no time to clean and disinfect the dirty utility room.	
You have a chest infection.	

key terms

PPE: personal protective equipment, for example a uniform, hats, gloves and aprons that create a barrier between the wearer and the vulnerable person or contaminated substance.

Standard precautions: practices such as wearing PPE and effective hand washing. If everyone practised these precautions, the risk of infections spreading would be reduced as far as it is reasonably possible to do so.

Ensuring visitors, residents and others follow good hygiene practices

The chief consideration for good hygiene is effective hand washing. However, there are some other basic practices to be aware of, such as avoiding direct contact with vulnerable people and not visiting people when you have an infection.

The wearing of disposable gloves and aprons or use of personal protective equipment (**PPE**) is a way of creating a barrier between you and the individual or a hazardous substance so that bacteria are prevented from spreading. These practices are known as **standard precautions**.

Strategies to promote hygiene

ACTIVITY

Task 2 of this activity will require you to use paper and coloured marker pens, or use the computer.

1. List as many things as you can think of to promote successful infection control procedures or practices in a care setting and compare your ideas to those of your colleagues.

2. Design a simple but effective poster to explain how visitors can contribute to 'standard precautions'.

Move and handle equipment and other objects safely

It is important to realise that injuries incurred through lifting heavy objects or people incorrectly can end up giving you a lifetime of pain and possibly stop you from working. Make sure you take part in adequate training so that you know how to lift people using the correct techniques and posture, so helping to prevent **musculoskeletal disorders.**

The main points of legislation that relate to safe moving and handling

key term

Musculoskeletal disorders: injury to muscles and bones, particularly in joints and the back.

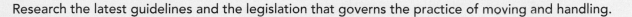

ACTIVITY

Research the latest guidelines and the legislation that governs the practice of moving and handling.

1. What do the guidelines require organisations to do?

2. What do you understand by the acronym TILE?

3. Look at the following example of a resident with a mobility issue and follow the steps of the risk assessment process to say how you would reduce the potential risk of injury, what you would use and what you would document in a care plan.

   To remind you here are the five steps of the risk assessment process.
   - ✿ Identify the hazards and associated risks.
   - ✿ Decide who might be harmed and how.
   - ✿ Evaluate the risks to determine what will reduce them.
   - ✿ Record the findings.
   - ✿ Monitor, review and revise.

Potential hazard

Alexios is a 53-year-old man who weighs 20 stone. He has a dry skin condition that means his skin is very fragile in some parts of his body. He needs to be lifted from his bed and into a large chair.

a. What are the risks?

b. Who may be harmed?

c. What equipment or resources could you access and what would be the checks? What principles of lifting would you use?

d. What information do you need to record?

e. What will you monitor and how will you review this?

There are many new resources and equipment available for lifting and transferring people and you might find this interesting to research. Try visiting www.rcn.org.uk for information on restraint or www.hse.gov.uk.

The principles of safe moving and handling

Poor moving and handling techniques continue to be the main cause of back injuries in health and social care work, even though equipment is used for lifting people or objects. Safe moving and handling techniques are included in induction training and regular annual updates and it is imperative that you attend these.

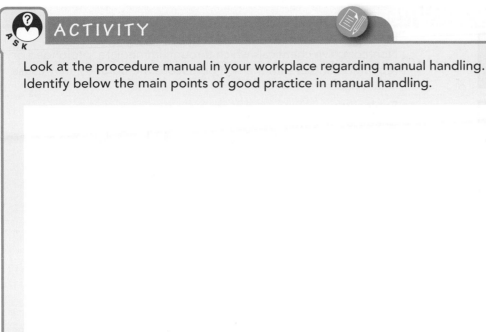

ACTIVITY

Look at the procedure manual in your workplace regarding manual handling. Identify below the main points of good practice in manual handling.

Handle hazardous substances and materials

Types of hazardous substances that may be found in the work setting

In order to handle substances, you need to be aware of how hazardous they are and know your workplace policy and procedures on using hazardous substances (or being in contact with them). You should also know how to dispose of them safely without risk of harming yourself, others or the environment.

The main hazardous substances classifications are shown in the following table.

Hazard symbol	Hazard classification
☠ T+ or T	**Very Toxic (T+) / Toxic (T)** Chemicals which in very low quantities cause death or acute or chronic damage to health when inhaled, swallowed or absorbed through the skin.
✗ Xn	**Harmful** Chemicals which may cause death or acute or chronic damage to health.
⚗ C	**Corrosive** Chemicals which on contact with living tissues may destroy them.

Hazard symbol	Hazard classification
Xi	**Irritant** Non-corrosive chemicals which through immediate, prolonged or repeated contact with the skin or mucous membranes, may cause inflammation.
E	**Explosive** Chemicals that may react producing heat without atmospheric oxygen, quickly producing gases and which can detonate and explode.
O	**Oxidising** Chemicals which give rise to heat producing reactions when in contact with other substances, particularly flammable substances.
F+ or F	**Flammable** **Extremely (F+)**: Liquids that have an extremely low flash point (below 0°C) and low boiling point (equal to or below 35°C). Or gaseous substances which are flammable in contact with air at ambient temperature and pressure. **Highly (F)**: Chemicals which may become hot and catch fire in contact with air at ambient temperature without any application of energy. A solid which readily catches fire with minimal contact with a source of ignition and which continue to burn after the source is removed. Liquids with a very low flashpoint (equal to or less than 21°C) and not classified as extremely flammable.

ASK ACTIVITY

Complete the following table by identifying two examples of each of the different hazardous substances.

Classification	Two examples of this type of hazardous substance
Very Toxic.	
Toxic.	
Harmful.	
Corrosive.	
Irritant.	
Explosive.	
Oxidising.	

Classification	Two examples of this type of hazardous substance
Extremely Flammable.	
Highly Flammable.	

ACTIVITY

1. A new worker is cleaning inside a cupboard after a leak from the U-bend under the sink. The cupboard contains bottles of cleaning fluids. The flood has made many of the bottles' labels damp and some of them have fallen off. She announces that she will mix the contents of one bottle with a small amount left in another that looks the same, as they are both nearly empty. However, the instructions on the labels are unreadable.

   Explain your response and how you would help her to understand the hazards of cleaning materials. Include a list of at least four detrimental effects of the cleaning materials being misused.

2. You are alarmed to discover soiled sheets covered in blood and urine on the floor in the dirty utility room. How will you explain to the new colleagues who left them there about the hazards of the soiled sheets?

Hazards found in the work setting

Safe practices for storing and using hazardous substances

ACTIVITY

Imagine you have just become the team leader and have decided to continue some induction training on COSHH for the new recruits who made mistakes in the previous activity.

Complete the table below to indicate what the potential hazard is, how the hazardous substance should be stored and the basic principles of using it safely. An example has been done for you.

Hazardous substance	Why it is hazardous and how it should be stored?	Principles for safe handling
Disinfectant.	Potential risks: can residents access these? Toxicity occurs from close storage. This is a biohazard and should be stored in a locked cupboard away from food and medications.	PPE: gloves and aprons. Follow the instructions on the label. Replace the cap tightly and place back in a locked cupboard.
Aerosol deodoriser (flammable).		
Medicines.		
Controlled drugs.		

Safe disposal of hazardous substances and materials

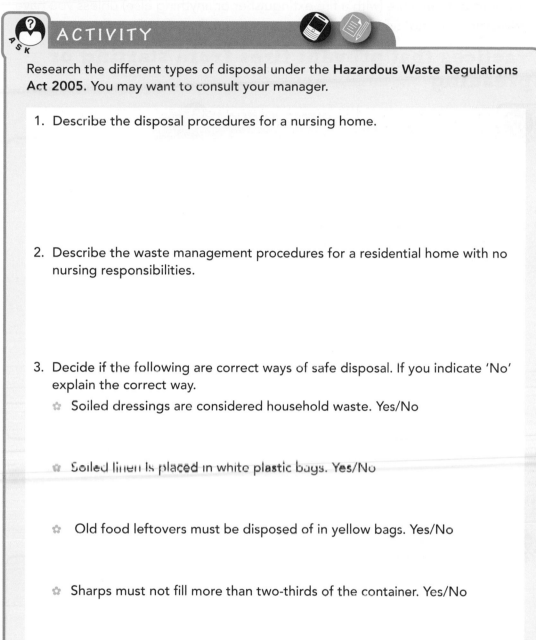

ACTIVITY

Research the different types of disposal under the **Hazardous Waste Regulations Act 2005**. You may want to consult your manager.

1. Describe the disposal procedures for a nursing home.

2. Describe the waste management procedures for a residential home with no nursing responsibilities.

3. Decide if the following are correct ways of safe disposal. If you indicate 'No' explain the correct way.
   * Soiled dressings are considered household waste. Yes/No

   * Soiled linen is placed in white plastic bags. Yes/No

   * Old food leftovers must be disposed of in yellow bags. Yes/No

   * Sharps must not fill more than two-thirds of the container. Yes/No

Assessor tip

You could describe safe practice for storing, using and disposing of hazardous substances while your assessor observes you undertaking each task.

Promote fire safety in the work setting

Under the Regulations Reform (Fire Safety) Order 2005, a responsible person (the employer) must carry out a fire risk assessment and put measures in place that protect all individuals to reduce the risk of fire as low as is 'reasonably practicable'. You should be fully aware of the fire alarm points, the equipment on site and its specific uses, as well as the evacuation plan including procedures for both able-bodied people and those with poor mobility. Your assembly point should be noted in all rooms and you should take the register and visitors' book with you when evacuating. Updating your knowledge and training is essential, but you must never attempt to put out a fire (with a fire extinguisher or anything else) unless you have received fire training. See www.communities.gov.uk/firesafety for more details.

Practices that prevent fires from starting or spreading

ACTIVITY

Make a list of all the issues you need to consider when conducting a fire risk assessment. Put as much detail as you can and compare your list with your friends and colleagues. An example has been done for you.

Fire doors closed.

Emergency procedures and ensuring that clear evacuation routes are maintained at all times

ACTIVITY

1. Explain what you need to do if you discover a fire, including the evacuation procedure.

2. Identify four types of fire extinguisher.

Understand the extinguishers in your organisation

Implement security measures in the work setting

You must be constantly aware of the possibility of intruders in the building who might intend to harm or steal. This can happen in the daytime as well as at night, so you must always check that visitors are there for a valid reason, are met in the entrance hall or lobby and are asked to sign a visitors' book. This is also to check, in the event of a fire, that all people on the premises are removed safely.

Procedures for checking identity and purpose of the visit

  ACTIVITY

Some visitors might get annoyed if you imply that they are possible intruders. However, if the procedures are applied equally to everyone, this eases the feeling of mistrust. The best way to do this is to put up a notice explaining why you need to check the identity and purpose of visit of all visitors, and why you have passwords or codes to enter the building.

You will need separate sheets of paper or use of a computer for this activity.

1. Design a positive security poster to display on the outside wall or in the vestibule, showing the reasons for the checks and the measures in place for security of the building and protection of the residents. Ensure your language is simple and reassuring.

2. Design a handout for new recruits on how to maintain their own safety and security, especially during night duty.

Keeping residents secure

As a team, you need to be aware of the residents who may wander and who become confused and forgetful at times.

Under the Mental Capacity Act 2007 and the Human Rights Act 1998 you cannot detain anyone in their rooms but you can support them in understanding their surroundings and keeping safe. It is also not compulsory to keep a private home locked but there should a system to protect people and property.

Another related issue arises when a resident does not wish to see a visitor, such as a particular family member.

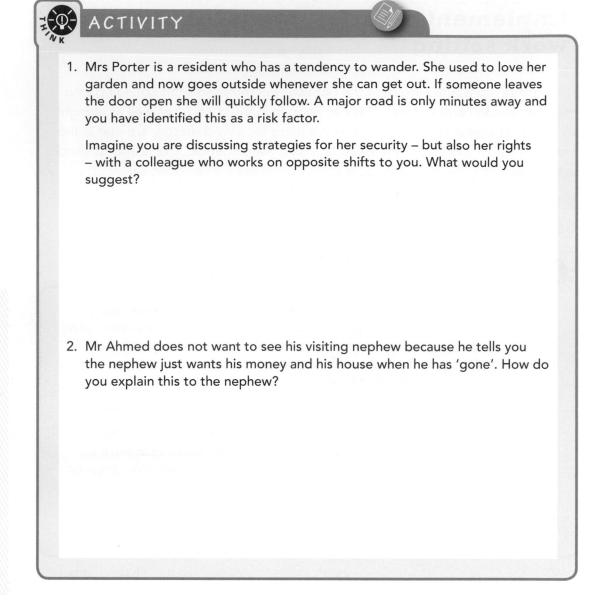

ACTIVITY

1. Mrs Porter is a resident who has a tendency to wander. She used to love her garden and now goes outside whenever she can get out. If someone leaves the door open she will quickly follow. A major road is only minutes away and you have identified this as a risk factor.

   Imagine you are discussing strategies for her security – but also her rights – with a colleague who works on opposite shifts to you. What would you suggest?

2. Mr Ahmed does not want to see his visiting nephew because he tells you the nephew just wants his money and his house when he has 'gone'. How do you explain this to the nephew?

Security in the work setting and the importance of ensuring that others are aware of own whereabouts

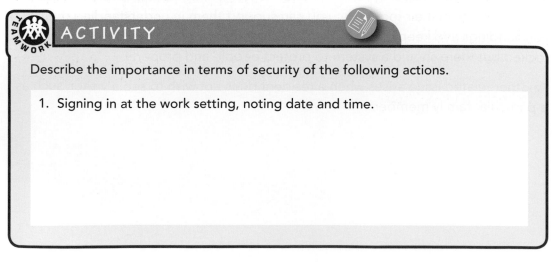

ACTIVITY

Describe the importance in terms of security of the following actions.

1. Signing in at the work setting, noting date and time.

2. Signing out at the end of a shift.

3. Phoning your line manager when you start a community visit and phoning again at the end of the visit.

4. Completing a daily schedule sheet to show duties and sites visited.

Know how to manage stress

'Stress' is a term that is sometimes used too lightly, indicating a busy time rather than a truly stressful time.

Stressors are issues that affect an individual in a psychological way initially but that can eventually affect someone physically in a negative way. Cortisone is released by the body when it is under stress and this can have negative effects on the immune system, making the individual more susceptible to illness and, sometimes, extreme tiredness. Another phrase sometimes lightly used is 'feeling under pressure' but this feeling can have serious effects on the mind and body. People sometimes say they are 'balancing too many plates 'or 'burning the candle at both ends'. If people are overstretched continually, this will have detrimental effects on their health and well-being.

key term

Stressors: anything that causes stress.

Balancing too many plates

The common signs and indicators of stress

ACTIVITY

Try to think of how you feel when you are feeling under pressure. Are you able to analyse the triggers that cause stress in your life?

Signs and indicators of stress can be divided into three categories:

- ✿ **physical signs and complaints**
- ✿ **cognitive signs**
- ✿ **behavioural signs.**

For each category in the table, enter as many signs and indicators as you can think of, and compare your list with those of your friends and colleagues.

Physical signs and complaints	Cognitive signs	Behavioural signs

Strategies for managing stress

ACTIVITY

Compare the findings in the previous activity and make a table to show the strategies that three of your friends or colleagues use to manage the warnings or triggers of stress, such as taking time out. Identify the common ideas.

Friends'/colleagues' stress triggers	Ways that these are managed

Sonia

CASE STUDY

Sonia has just returned to work in a nursing and residential home after a career break. She tells you she is finding it difficult to cope with all the changes in her life and her shifts mean that she is getting tired and not managing her home life and three children as well as she thought she would.

A few weeks later you are working together again and you notice that she appears anxious and irritable and is reluctant to do any tasks. You ask her if she is feeling well but she replies sharply that she is perfectly fine. You are puzzled that she is no longer open with you and not performing her duties as she should be.

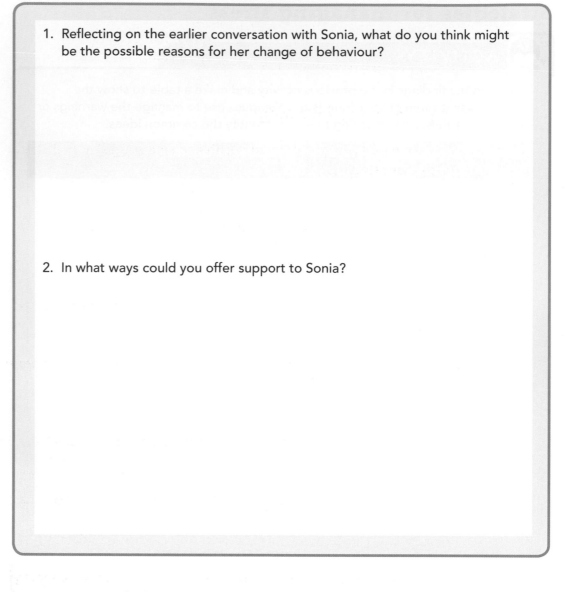

1. Reflecting on the earlier conversation with Sonia, what do you think might be the possible reasons for her change of behaviour?

2. In what ways could you offer support to Sonia?

It is important to find someone at work who you feel able to talk to and who will help you manage any work-related stress, as you may be in breach of confidentiality to discuss work matters outside the workplace. Stress related to work can only be resolved through things changing at work, and this can only occur if advice and support are sought through your employer. They may provide a confidential service to provide advice and support.

ARE YOU READY FOR ASSESSMENT?

☑ **Do you know the following:**

☐ 1. The main points of the general health and safety legislation that applies to health and social care settings?

☐ 2. The main responsibilities that you, your employer and others in the work setting have in relation to health and safety?

☐ 3. The work tasks that require special training before you can carry them out?

☐ 4. The different types of accidents and sudden illnesses that can happen in your work setting and what to do if they occur?

☐ 5. Your role in supporting others to follow practices that reduce the spread of infection?

☐ 6. The legislation and principles that apply to moving and handling equipment and objects safely?

☐ 7. The hazardous substances and materials found in your work setting?

☐ 8. How to prevent fires starting and spreading?

☐ 9. The procedures to follow in the event of a fire?

☐ 10. The reasons for ensuring others know of your whereabouts while you are in the workplace?

☐ 11. The common signs and indicators of stress?

☐ 12. The signs that indicate your own stress, your stress triggers and how to manage these?

☑ **Can you do the following:**

☐   **1.** Use policies and procedures or other agreed ways of working that relate to health and safety and minimise potential risks and hazards?

☐   **2.** Support others to understand and follow safe practices?

☐   **3.** Monitor and report potential health and safety risks?

☐   **4.** Use risk assessment in relation to health and safety?

☐   **5.** Minimise potential risks and hazards?

☐   **6.** Access additional support regarding health and safety?

☐   **7.** Wash your hands according to the recommended procedure?

☐   **8.** Ensure your own health and hygiene standards at work do not pose a risk to others?

☐   **9.** Safely move and handle equipment and other objects?

☐   **10.** Safely store, use and dispose of hazardous substances and materials?

☐   **11.** Take measures to prevent fires from starting?

☐   **12.** Keep evacuation routes clear and safe for use in an emergency?

☐   **13.** Check the identity of anyone wishing to access your workplace or information?

☐   **12.** Take appropriate action to ensure you and others in your workplace are safe and secure?

UNIT HSC 038

Promote good practice in handling information in health and social care settings

This unit will help you to understand your role and responsibilities, and those of others, in promoting and maintaining good practice in handling information within a health and social care setting. The activities will support your knowledge and awareness to help you to monitor your practices in terms of recording, sharing, storing and accessing information.

You must work within a legal framework and this unit informs you of how you must follow organisational procedures that comply with this framework. It also addresses the maintenance and security of records and supporting others in keeping records secure.

You will need to be able to:
- ✿ understand requirements for handling information in health and social care settings
- ✿ implement good practice in handling information
- ✿ support others to handle information.

Requirements for handling information in health and social care settings

You will need to have a basic knowledge of the relevant legislation that governs information handling. It is therefore a good idea for you to research the following legislation and codes of practice for the first few activities.

✿ The Data Protection Act 1998
✿ The Freedom of Information Act 2000
✿ The Access to Health Records 1990
✿ The NHS Confidentiality Code of Practice
✿ The Human Rights Act 1990
✿ **Common law of confidentiality**
✿ The Health and Social Care Act 2008 (Regulated Activities) Regulations 2010
✿ The Care Quality Commission (Registration) Regulations 2009

key term

Common law of confidentiality: a common understanding that the information you pass on to a doctor, for example, will be kept confidential.

Legislation and codes of practice

ACTIVITY

Read the following statements that define an aspect of a certain Act or code of practice related to the handling of information.

Draw a line from the statement to the correct Act or code of practice.

Statement	Act or code of practice
A person who has a right to make a claim for negligence on another person's behalf can access personal data if the person concerned has died.	The NHS Confidentiality Code of Practice
A person has rights to an opinion, to receive information and impart ideas and information freely, but must do so with restraint for confidential issues.	The Data Protection Act 1998
Anyone collecting information must process this for a limited and specifically stated purpose.	Access to Health Records 1990
Decisions about whether to disclose information must be made on a case-by-case basis.	Freedom of Information Act 2000
Anyone has the right to request information held by public sector organisations and to receive it within 20 working days.	The Health and Social Care Act and CQC
Information disclosed to a doctor is generally considered confidential.	The Human Rights Act 1990
Records must be kept up to date, legible, accurate, signed and dated.	Common law of confidentiality

Legal requirements and codes of practice for handling information

The Code of Practice for Social Care Workers was developed in 2001 by the General Social Care Council. It is a list of statements describing a set of standards that social care workers should adhere to in order to promote and maintain a high standard of care (www.gscc.org.uk). There is also a set of standards for employers of social care workers.

The sections relevant to handling information are:

✿ 2.3 You must respect confidential information and clearly explain agency policies about confidentiality to service users and carers

✿ 3.2 You must use established processes and procedures to challenge and report dangerous, abusive, discriminatory or exploitative behaviour and practice

✿ 5.3 You must not abuse the trust of service users and carers or the access you have to personal information about them or to their property, home or workplace

✿ 5.8 You must not behave in a way in work or outside work that would call into question your suitability to work in social care services

✿ 6.2 You must maintain clear and accurate records as required by procedures established for your work.

The CQC (Care Quality Commission) use these standards when conducting an **audit trail**.

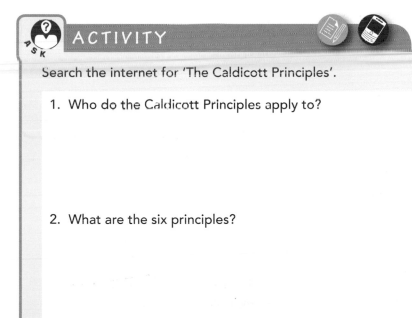

ACTIVITY

Search the internet for 'The Caldicott Principles'.

1. Who do the Caldicott Principles apply to?

2. What are the six principles?

key term

Audit trail: evidence of good standards observed by examining records.

Recording information

CASE STUDY

You are working in the community and meet Mrs Wall, who needs help with personal care. As you are chatting, she tells you that she has felt very nervous of her daughter-in-law visiting, who she is convinced is stealing her money.

1. What is your immediate response?

2. Describe what your next actions would be.

3. Explain how your actions comply with the above statements and the Code of Practice for Social Care Workers.

How would you respond?

Essential Standards of Quality and Safety

The Essential Standards of Quality and Safety consist of 28 regulations (and associated outcomes) that are set out in two pieces of legislation:

* the Health and Social Care Act 2008 (Regulated Activities) Regulations 2010
* the Care Quality Commission (Registration) Regulations 2009.

There is an associated outcome for each regulation, that is, the experiences we expect people to have as a result of the care they receive. During an inspection there must be evidence that care services meet these outcomes.

The outcomes related to information handling are as follows.

* **Regulation 18 (Outcome 2):** People give consent to their care and treatment and understand and know how to change decisions about things that have been agreed previously.

* **Regulation 19 (Outcome 17):** People, and those acting on their behalf, have their comments and complaints listened to and acted on effectively and know that they will not be discriminated against for making a complaint.

The above two outcomes involve the recording of a changed decision and any complaints.

✿ **Regulation 20 (Outcome 2):** People's personal records are accurate, fit for purpose, held securely and remain confidential. The same applies to other records that are needed to protect safety and well-being.

Essential standards

ACTIVITY

Read the following scenarios and:

✿ identify the relevant outcome from those listed above that each situation relates to

✿ decide how you would pass on this information, and to whom

✿ consider what needs to be recorded.

1. Mr McMarne has had his medication changed since his recent dizzy spells and breathlessness. He now complains to you that one of the tablets he takes is making him worse.

2. Mrs Holloway discovered that she is pregnant and she has requested a termination of pregnancy without her husband knowing.

3. Thomas is 22 and has been diagnosed as HIV-positive. He is in a new relationship with a young man and informs you that he is not going to tell him.

Assessor tip

You will be showing your assessor your competence in handling information whenever you access records and record information. You can show them your understanding of the legal and organisational requirements if you provide an explanation as they observe you undertaking these activities.

Your questions answered...

If people are not able to give consent for keeping information, what should I do?

This refers to Regulation 18 (Outcome 2) noted on page 182:

'People give consent to their care and treatment and understand and know how to change decisions about things that have been agreed previously'.

If consent is difficult to obtain, the individual can appoint a representative (often a close relative or friend) to make decisions for them. This is called a 'lasting power of attorney'. If no one is given this power, a health care professional can make the judgements. You must seek advice from your manager.

Implement good practice in handling information

Legal requirements for recording: the Data Protection Act

key term

Processing of data: obtaining, recording, holding, altering, retrieving and destroying or disclosing data or information.

The Data Protection Act lays down strict conditions for the **processing of data**, with more stringent rules for sensitive information related to race, ethnic origin, sexual choices, and sexual or mental health.

The Act states that anyone collecting information for any kind of processing must follow eight principles.

1. Fairly and lawfully process it.

2. Process it only for limited, specifically stated purposes.

3. Use it in an adequate and relevant way – not excessively.

4. Use it accurately.

5. Keep it on file no longer than necessary.

6. Process it in accordance with legal rights.

7. Keep it secure.

8. Never transfer it outside the UK without adequate protection.

Lawful processing requires compliance with the common law of confidentiality.

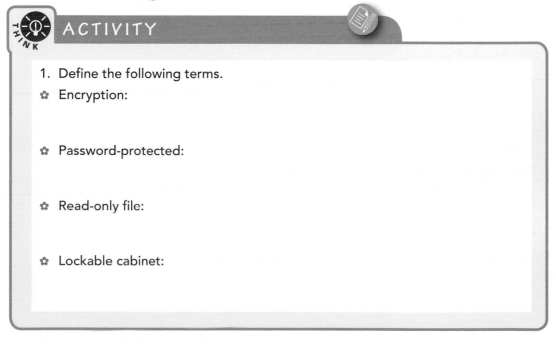

ACTIVITY

Complete the gaps in the following passage using the words below.

opinion   illegal   explain   permission   specialist   treatment
personal   health care   purpose   senior   third   individual

When you enter _____ details into a computer system, you will need to obtain

_____ from the _____ after explaining the _____ of keeping

this on file. If the information relates to a diagnosis or _____, you will need to

_____ that it may be necessary to seek the _____ of others, for example a

_____, to determine better ways to treat a condition.

Information is given to a _____ party, usually with the aim of improving

_____ _____, but it may be necessary to inform the police, for example if information

given to you is _____ in its context. If you suspect this, you must seek advice from a

_____ before making your report.

Manual and electronic systems to secure the storage of information

The Data Protection Act is chiefly concerned with information that is stored electronically.

Accessing information stored on a computer can be risky if it is not held securely. You would not want to publicise your bank details to everybody and, if you do not use password-protected schemes, anyone can access the information stored.

Secure storage

ACTIVITY

1. Define the following terms.

✿ Encryption:

✿ Password-protected:

✿ Read-only file:

✿ Lockable cabinet:

✿ Ciphers:

✿ Shredder:

✿ CCTV:

✿ Safe:

✿ Intranet:

✿ Backed up:

✿ Smartcard:

2. Which of the above relate to paper-based files and which relate to electronic files?

3. What essential information can be shown when electronic reports are used, rather than paper-based ones?

4. Describe two or three advisable guidelines for setting passwords.

Maintain records that are complete, up to date and accurate

When writing a report, you need to ensure that it conforms to good practice guidelines, so that it can be understood and acted on by others. A poor report may result in a negative outcome on the individual concerned, as inappropriate care could harm them. It is essential that you:

* write in clear, formal language
* use correct grammar, spelling and punctuation. If you use a computer, word-processing software can help you with this
* include only the facts, as accurately as possible, and not your personal thoughts and feelings or any personal remarks about people described in your report
* don't include any jargon, slang or phrases that people outside your setting may not understand
* remember that people described within the report usually have a right to access what has been written about them. Bearing this in mind can help you to decide how to phrase the report.

It is very important to keep your report writing to the point, accurate and **objective**. Date and sign all your records in (if written by hand) black ink with no correction fluid (this can make records look as if they have been tampered with). If errors occur, you need to cross them out and initial your error.

key term

Objective: what you see and hear, not what you assume to be the meaning, which is deemed to exist only in your mind (subjective).

ACTIVITY

Find a written report you have recently completed. Using the good practice guidance on writing reports given above, analyse your report.

1. What examples do you think there are of good practice in your report?

2. Ask your line manager to look at your report and identify examples of good practice. Compare the two. Have you both identified the same examples or different examples?

3. Which areas of report writing do you need to improve?

4. Who and what can help you with your report-writing skills?

5. How will you monitor and review the improvements in your report writing?

Poor report writing

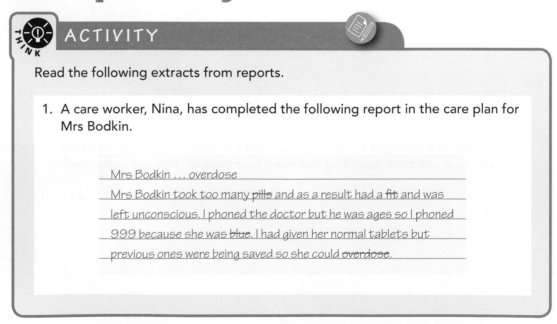

ACTIVITY

Read the following extracts from reports.

1. A care worker, Nina, has completed the following report in the care plan for Mrs Bodkin.

> Mrs Bodkin … overdose
>
> Mrs Bodkin took too many pills and as a result had a ~~fit~~ and was
>
> left unconscious. I phoned the doctor but he was ages so I phoned
>
> 999 because she was ~~blue~~. I had given her normal tablets but
>
> previous ones were being saved so she could ~~overdose~~.

The report was written in pencil with several crossings out. Explain the problems with the writing and presentation and rewrite the report yourself.

2. Susan, another care worker, has completed the following report in the care plan for Mr Allinson.

> Mr Allinson ... rubbish
>
> Mr Allinson has had a nasty rash for days and now says he is
>
> going home because we do not treat him properly. His daughter
>
> has told my colleague that the night staff are rubbish.
>
> Date:
>
> Signature:

This report was written in pen, and several mistakes have been covered in correction fluid. Explain the problems with the writing and presentation and rewrite the report yourself.

3. Describe at least four professional standards to consider when recording notes.

Support others to handle information

You will need to explain to others the reasons for careful report writing and storing of information. 'Others' can mean relatives, visitors, residents, patients, colleagues and health professionals.

Support others to understand the need for secure handling of information

ACTIVITY

Imagine you are caring for Mr McMarne. He was the individual in the earlier activity who has had his medication changed since his recent dizzy spells and breathlessness (see page 183). He has complained to you that one of the tablets he takes is making him worse. One night he becomes increasingly agitated.

You decide to call the GP. He is aware of Mr McMarne and he asks you to change his medication and to give him something else.

What are the guidelines for acting on verbal information? Find out the procedure for this and state what must be done as soon as possible to ensure the safety and security of the handling of information.

Support others to understand and contribute to records

All care staff will have training and induction into the safe handling of information in accordance with the organisation's policy and procedures. This usually involves staff members holding a username and password or a smartcard giving access to a computer that stores information.

You are responsible for the maintenance of confidential reports and accountable for your actions regarding these.

Security measures

ACTIVITY

Complete the gaps in the following passage using the words below to highlight your responsibilities in maintaining the security of accessing information.

uncertain shredder paper-based senior staff records accessing
procedures purpose personal identity health evidence

✿ It is important to ensure new _____ and visiting _____ professionals are aware of the _____ for _____ information held on the computer. Your organisation may have procedures for recording details of who is accessing information and for what _____. It will also be important for you to be absolutely sure of their _____.

✿ Visiting health professionals should carry some _____ of this. If you are _____ of this, contact your _____ before that person has any access to _____.

✿ If _____-_____ notes are entered in a computer system and you are asked to destroy them you must do this using a _____ to eradicate all _____ details.

Sharing relevant information

You need to be aware of the circumstances that allow information to be shared. Although the law gives people the right to confidentiality, as well as protection under the Data Protection Act and privacy under the Human Rights Act, these are not absolute rights and need to be balanced with those of others. It could be beneficial for the public to know some information, for example, about outbreaks of flu or meningitis.

Under certain circumstances some information in a personal file will be withheld from the individual it concerns. This is generally the case when that information is considered by relevant professionals to be harmful.

The National Information Governance Board for Health and Social Care (www. nigb.nhs.uk) gives special permission to share information about individuals without consent. These include registers of births and deaths and reporting gunshot wounds to the police.

Sharing information

ACTIVITY

1. Explain four reasons why information should be shared. Relate your answers to the people in the activity on page 183 (Mr McMarne, Mrs Holloway and Thomas).

2. Research and describe the role of a 'Caldicott Guardian'.

Night shift

CASE STUDY

You are working a night shift on a small unit caring for eight people with mental health issues as well an annexe that houses four residents with dementia. You have one senior care worker and another health care assistant. You are new to the provision and this is your first night shift. You find that some residents are more restless at night and that the three of you are not ensuring the full safety of everyone in the care provision. There is someone calling out so you and one colleague go to attend to the resident, but the other worker has gone for a break and you think the other residents are vulnerable.

1. With whom do you share this information?

2. What facts should be reported?

3. What essential standards are being compromised?

ARE YOU READY FOR ASSESSMENT?

☑ **Do you know the following:**

☐ **1.** The main points of the legislation that applies to recording, storing and sharing information in health and social care settings?

☐ **2.** The features of manual and electronic information storage systems that help to ensure security?

☑ **Can you do the following:**

☐ **1.** Work in ways that maintain security when accessing and storing information?

☐ **2.** Keep up-to-date, complete, accurate and legible records?

☐ **3.** Support others to understand the need to handle information securely?

☐ **4.** Support others to understand and contribute to records?

UNIT DEM 301

Understand the process and experience of dementia

This unit will help you to understand how the brain is affected by dementia so you can appreciate the difficulties that sufferers experience. It will enable you to gain a better overall understanding of behaviours associated with dementia and so you will be able to support those difficulties and adjust your own behaviour.

You will need to be able to:

* understand the neurology of dementia
* understand the impact of recognition and diagnosis of dementia
* understand how dementia care must be underpinned by a person-centred approach.

The neurology of dementia

The range of causes of dementia syndrome

It is essential for you to understand how the brain works in order to appreciate the many types of difficulties that people with dementia experience. The exact cause of dementia is not known, but research has shown that there are different variations of the condition. Our knowledge of the brain shows that irreversible damage of the areas contained within the brain has specific impacts on people's behaviours, emotions, personality, social interactions, movements, memory and reasoning skills. Damage to the right side of the brain affects the left side of the body and vice versa.

The brain is divided into two hemispheres (halves) each containing four areas (lobes). This structure is called the cerebrum. At the base of the cerebrum sits a smaller structure called the cerebellum.

These areas are interconnected by nerve cells called neurones. Neurones send and receive messages to all parts of the body as well as within the brain.

Deep in the brain there are other structures that may become affected by dementia. These are the hippocampus, the amygdala, the hypothalamus and the limbic system.

ACTIVITY

1. Look at the diagram of the brain below and label the correct lobe using the information provided. You may have to research this.

Lobes: Frontal lobe
          Parietal lobe
          Temporal lobe
          Occipital lobe

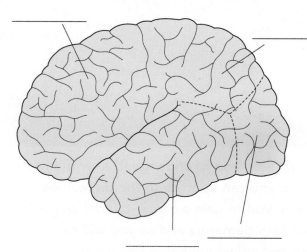

2. Now place the correct lobe with the correct function.

✿ The _____ lobe is concerned with learning new tasks, memory, reasoning and motivation.

✿ The _____ lobe is known as the visual centre.

✿ The _____ lobe controls language and information processing.

✿ The _____ lobe controls hearing, short-term memory processing and speech.

3. What part of the brain deals with motor co-ordination?

The types of memory impairment commonly experienced by individuals with dementia

 ACTIVITY

1. Research the brain areas that have different effects on the function of the brain. In the second column of the table below, write the effects of impairment, and in the third column give one example of a difficulty this may create in the daily activities of the affected person. An example has been done for you.

Brain area	Damage	Example of difficulty
Frontal lobe.	Inability to plan or reason. Also affects the personality.	Thinking about things logically, such as problems getting dressed.
Temporal lobe.		
Parietal lobe.		
Occipital lobe.		
Cerebellum.		

2. How would you best support the difficulty in each case? Give an example, using an aspect of personal care or an activity that you can do to help. An example has been done for you.

Frontal lobe: Support the person by passing the correct item of clothing to them.

Temporal lobe:

Parietal lobe:

Occipital lobe:

Cerebellum:

3. Explain how factors that may not be attributable to dementia can cause changes in an individual's condition.

4. Explain why the abilities and needs of an individual with dementia may fluctuate.

Types of dementia

ACTIVITY

1. Look at the types of dementia identified in the left-hand column and match with the causes and descriptions in the right-hand column. Please note this list is not exhaustive and there are other, less common, causes of dementia. You will find the Alzheimer's Society website a good source of information, as it has a number of factsheets about the different types of dementia and the impact on individuals and their families. Look at www.alzheimers.org.uk.

Types of dementia	Causes and descriptions
Alzheimer's disease	Accounts for 55 per cent of all cases of dementia, and causes shrinkage of brain tissue and death of brain cells. Consists of neurofibrillary tangles and amyloid plaques.
Vascular dementia	Abnormalities of small clusters of protein that are thought to contribute to the death of brain cells.
Pick's disease	Accounts for 20 per cent of cases and occurs as a result of problems with blood supply, usually strokes.
Dementia with Lewy bodies	Slow, progressive type of dementia that affects younger people's behaviour and control of emotions.

2. From your research, name two other types of dementia and write a sentence describing their cause and characteristics.

3. Give a brief summary of how caring for an individual with a progressive form may be different from caring for someone who has sustained damage in one area following a stroke.

From your research you will have found out that dementia is a long-term condition that mainly affects people over the age of 65 years, although some forms can affect people much younger than this. Dementia covers a range of symptoms, the combination of which depends on the specific type of dementia and parts of the brain affected.

How individuals process information with reference to the abilities and limitations of dementia

Several types of memory impairments may occur and these will affect the activities required for daily living. Damage that occurs in the brain can affect thinking and the processing of information.

The hippocampus, the amygdala, the hypothalamus and the limbic system play a part in the memory and emotions. These structures are deep within the brain. Dementia starts by affecting the outer layer of the brain and the deeper structures are affected later, so very poor memory and information processing is thought to be a late-stage development.

In the case of a vascular dementia (caused by strokes), the damage is confined to the area affected by a bleed or clot in the brain. In Alzheimer's disease the damage is slower, affecting a larger area. It is also progressive, so memory problems worsen as time goes on.

Activities such as driving a car or going shopping are learned skills that most of us take for granted. They are usually developed and remembered quite easily, but any damage to the brain could mean that these skills and memories are diminished and – in the case of Alzheimer's disease – eventually forgotten altogether.

Noting changes

ACTIVITY

You may have cared for people with dementia or read about it in the past. What sort of memory problems will be experienced? How can you and your colleagues, as a team, observe changes in someone's memory and thinking?

Read below the daily routine of Allie, who has started to experience short-term memory loss. In the second column indicate the difficulties she may experience with each daily activity now or in the future. An example has been done for you.

Daily activity	Possible difficulty with memory loss: Initially/Later
Wakes and makes a cup of tea.	Initially: cannot remember where the tea bags or the sugar are kept. Later: not able to fill the kettle, boil the water or place the tea in a cup.
Switches on the radio and listens while drinking tea.	
Gets washed and dressed.	

Daily activity	Possible difficulty with memory loss: Initially/Later
Makes breakfast, usually toast and more tea.	
Walks to the bus stop and catches a bus to town.	

Processing information

When we receive information, we need to process it: to understand it and store it. We then need to retrieve it for later use. Problems may occur at any stage of this process (receiving and understanding, storing and retrieving). When we hear something or learn something new, we register that information and our brain stores it as short-term memory on the surface of the temporal lobes.

There is increasing evidence to suggest that people with Alzheimer's disease experience significant changes to their visual function. It has been found that the changes relate to the individual's clarity of vision: their ability to discern different levels of light, and ability to see colours and view things in three dimensions. The presence of eye conditions, as well as hearing loss or impairment, will affect the ability to process information. It is important, therefore, to ensure that sensory impairments are considered and, if possible, remedied, as this will increase the individual's ability to process information and communicate with others.

 ACTIVITY

Allie (from the previous activity) has deteriorated and is now in a residential unit. She is 87, has impaired vision and hearing but is very mobile and sociable.

Yesterday Allie's niece visited her and today you ask Allie how the visit went. She says she's never had a visitor and when you say, 'Yes, Allie, your niece came', she appears to get agitated and upset.

Why is Allie upset?

1. Why does Allie become upset?

2. What processes are occurring in Allie's brain to cause her loss of memory?

3. Describe three stages of information processing.

How other factors can cause changes in an individual's condition and why abilities may fluctuate

It is important to be aware of signs and symptoms that do not necessarily indicate that the dementia is worsening. A person with age-related memory impairment, while finding remembering things more difficult, will continue to recognise people, places and objects even though they may be unable to actually name them. If the individual has depression, they may also exhibit similar signs to dementia and so this needs to be excluded as a possible cause of changes in their well-being.

Think about how someone with an infection might feel and behave; most likely they will be despondent and possibly drowsy, which can also be signs of dementia.

ACTIVITY

Allie has recently been diagnosed with Alzheimer's disease and, as you monitor her condition, you notice some of her symptoms are getting worse, such as confusion, agitation and **receptive dysphasia**.

1. Explain other possible reasons for the worsening of her symptoms.

2. Explain how you might manage instructions with someone with receptive dysphasia.

3. Why might someone with a dementia resulting from a stroke be more depressed than a person with a progressive form of dementia, such as Alzheimer's disease?

4. Who would you ask for advice to support the people in your care?

5. Why might Allie's signs and symptoms fluctuate?

key term

Receptive dysphasia: failing to understand the spoken word.

Assessor tip

You will find it easier to understand and learn about dementia if you can relate it to the experiences of real people. If you are working with people with dementia, talk to them and their relatives about their experiences. If you are not currently working with people with dementia, read or listen to personal stories about how dementia affects the individual. These are available either as books or via the internet. This will help you to remember complex information when explaining dementia to your assessor.

The impact of recognition and diagnosis of dementia

Reporting and recording possible signs of dementia

Reporting and recording possible signs of dementia should be in accordance with your organisation's recording procedures. You may also find it useful to consider the following questions to help you provide sufficient detail and to keep your report factual:

* Provide evidence to support your findings, for example what did you actually see or hear? Or what is reported by others?

* Provide information to place the behaviour in context, for example the time of day. Does this behaviour only happen at a particular time of day or does it happen at any time? What other activity was occurring at that time? How frequently does the behaviour occur, does it happen occasionally or frequently during the day and is it every day?

Finding out that you have a progressive illness is a great shock, and to discover that the illness will affect you both mentally and physically is an even bigger shock.

Many emotions experienced after a diagnosis are difficult to deal with, and the person will need an enormous amount of support.

Mr Crawthorne

CASE STUDY

Mr Crawthorne is 68 years old and lives with his wife in a three-bedroomed house in a rural area. His retirement two years ago gave him a sense of freedom to enjoy his life and he has managed it well. He is a very active man, enjoying swimming, cycling, golf, reading and gardening. He and his wife also enjoy going away on holiday, shopping and eating out at different restaurants. He likes to take his grandchildren out and is in good health. However, he was shocked to receive the diagnosis that he has a progressive form of dementia and this has caused much anguish for both Mr Crawthorne and his wife.

Mr Crawthorne is shocked by his diagnosis

1. Expand on the possible emotions that contribute to the anguish felt by Mr Crawthorne and his wife.

2. How do you think his diagnosis will affect Mr Crawthorne's quality of life and everyday activities?

3. What information and advice do you think Mr and Mrs Crawthorne will need at this time?

4. How do you think Mrs Crawthorne's needs will differ from those of her husband?

5. Describe three or four sources of support that are available for both Mr Crawthorne and his wife.

6. Give two examples of what needs to be recorded and monitored and how these records should be stored.

The impact of receiving a diagnosis of dementia on the individual and their family and friends

You may find it particularly helpful to research the work of Dr Tom Kitwood about a diagnosis of dementia. He suggested that high quality social care involves ensuring that, along with basic health care, five psychosocial needs are met. These psychosocial needs are:

✿ comfort (responding to the wishes of the person for whatever makes them comfortable)

✿ attachment (ensuring family, friends and loved ones are involved in the care)

- inclusion (to encourage the person in doing activities with friends and carrying on minor tasks that they can manage)
- occupation (to be engaged in activities so they are occupied, experiencing positive interactions)
- identity (to retain their own individualism and to be treated as an individual).

If these needs are interlinked and applied continuously the person will be more settled.

Special support

ACTIVITY

Read again about Mr Crawthorne's life from the case study on page 204 and complete the table with him in mind, thinking of what he enjoys now and how he might fear for the future.

For each psychosocial need listed in the first column, give an example in the second column of what you think that particular psychosocial need means to Mr Crawthorne. Please note there may be an overlap of your possible answers. Use the third column to indicate how carers and his family can support him. An example has been done for you.

Psychosocial need	Example of the psychosocial need as it relates to Mr Crawthorne	Example of supporting strategy by carer or family
Comfort.	The accommodation he enjoys, his life with his wife and family and the comfort of his routine.	Assessment of needs (needs analysis), provision of required services but fine tuning this so that services respond to his personal likes and dislikes.
Attachment.		
Inclusion.		
Occupation.		

Psychosocial need	Example of the psychosocial need as it relates to Mr Crawthorne	Example of supporting strategy by carer or family
Identity.		

When recording possible signs of dementia, it important to report actual behaviour and not your interpretation of that behaviour. Dates and times may also be significant, as symptoms and signs may fluctuate during the course of the day. Reporting other significant factors that occurred before and after an incident may also be helpful in confirming a diagnosis or excluding other causes.

How dementia care must be underpinned by a person-centred approach

What is a person-centred approach?

Put simply, this means putting the person first and the dementia second.

Understanding a person fully also means understanding what they do and do not like to experience. Essentially, this is a focus on the individual's abilities, strengths and enjoyments, so that the person experiences a sense of well-being.

This focus is called adopting a 'strengths-based approach' and it allows for freedom of choice, dignity, independence and management of tasks at an individual's own pace.

Person-centred versus non-person-centred approach

<aside>
key term

Strengths-based approach: delivering care to focus on the strengths and positive activities that the person is able to do, not what they are unable to do.
</aside>

CASE STUDY

Eric is a care worker in a residential unit, and Harry, who is very slow in his movements is one of the residents. Harry's speech is a little slurred and he is very forgetful and confused when dressing and then finding his way to the dining room. He tends to repeat himself a lot and appears restless. Today, Eric enters the room in his usual hurried style and starts to find clothes for Harry to help him get dressed, because Harry cannot decide what he wants to wear. Eric is chatty but appears not to listen to Harry, who is very agitated. Eric says, 'Come on, we need to get a move on or your breakfast will get cold, Harry', and starts to tidy around him. Harry starts to shout and become angry, refusing to go with Eric.

Eric ends up shouting back at him, 'Oh well, don't have breakfast then this morning. Stay in your room until you have calmed down!'

1. Why do you think Harry began to shout?

2. How should Eric have behaved? Give your reasons.

3. If this behaviour is noted for the first time, what needs to be reported in the care plan?

Techniques to meet the fluctuating abilities and needs of the individual

Different techniques can be used to support the **physical environment** and also the social and emotional needs of the person.

The environment

ACTIVITY

Suggest ways of ensuring the spaces listed in the first column can be more welcoming and safe for people with dementia. Perhaps you are artistic and can design a very good purpose-built home!

Remember that people are likely to have other impairments, such as poor vision, hearing and mobility. Try to think of these impairments when you complete the table. Also think of what is pleasing to the eye and calming, as this is thought to help people with dementia. An example has been done for you.

Physical environment	Useful and safe features	Features for pleasure and stimulus
Personal room.	All fixed furniture if possible. Easy access around the bed space, rails if necessary and good lighting. Call system for help. En-suite toilet and wash area. Good natural light and ventilation.	Personal photos and photograph albums, pictures and paintings, crafts by grandchildren, a television and games that are enjoyed, for example jigsaws.

Physical environment	Useful and safe features	Features for pleasure and stimulus
En-suite wash facility/ toilet.		
Communal rooms and corridors.		
Gardens and paths.		

ACTIVITY

Research reality-orientation and validation. These are two techniques that are used with individuals with dementia to meet their fluctuating needs and abilities. Complete the table below by comparing the main points of each approach.

Main points of a reality-orientation approach	Main points of a validation approach

Emotions

 ACTIVITY

Think of the personal histories of people with a dementia and how to involve family and friends in providing the kind of activities that will promote their well-being and a sense of contentment. This activity focuses on the psychosocial needs of the person. Think of what you can offer in a residential home or a day care centre that would be stimulating, enjoyable and create happy emotional memories. See how creative and different you can be, but do remember this is up to the person you are caring for and not what you would like to do. An example has been done for you.

Emotional/Social needs	Example of these	Benefits for the person
Assistive technology.	Telephones with large numbers.	Able to see the numbers and contact people.
Reminiscence therapy, music and radio.		
Gardening.		
Baking.		
Exercise.		
Involving family and friends.		

Your questions answered...

Why is it important for carers to engage in conversations and activities with people with a dementia when these are never remembered or perhaps understood?

Emotional memory sits deep within the brain and it is the enjoyment of a conversation that is remembered more than the content – so carry on engaging in positive, happy and meaningful conversations and activities.

ACTIVITY

Identify different ways in which the social environment can encourage positive interactions with individuals with dementia. An example has been done for you.

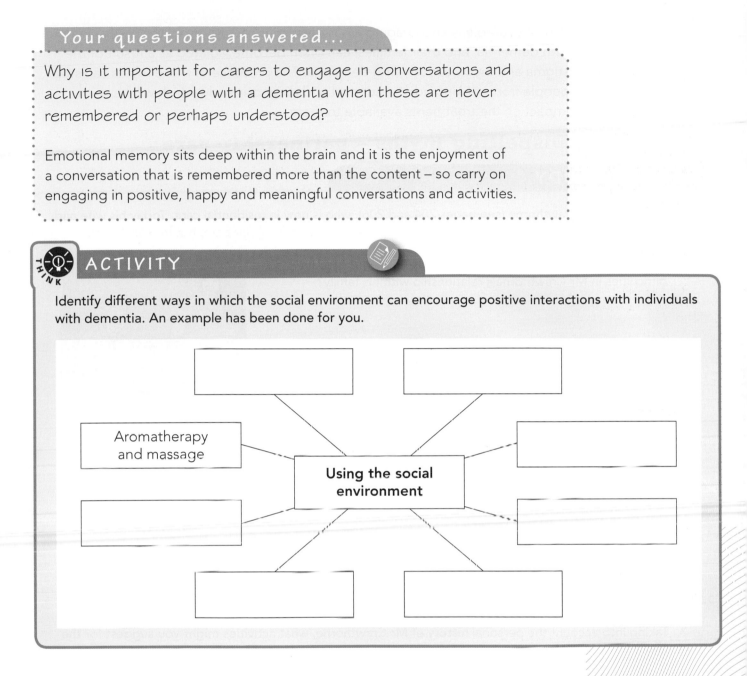

Myths and stereotypes

It is important to remain positive when caring for others with a dementia. Always remember that a person with dementia might experience negativity on a daily basis so you must retain your empathy in order to deliver good quality care.

The general public often have in mind a negative picture when dementia is mentioned. There have been many incidents of poor care practice shown on TV, which is rarely balanced with stories of care given to a high standard. Many people are led to believe that people with a dementia become 'cabbage-like' and cannot be supported at all but only 'managed'. There is often a belief that individuals with dementia are unable to make decisions for themselves, are unable to communicate with others or to care for themselves. In fact, people with dementia often manage well and live alone for a long time after their initial diagnosis, especially if the disease progression is slow.

Part of your role is encouraging a partnership of care to dispel the myths. People with dementia, and their families, can often become isolated as a result of the stigma and myths surrounding dementia. The presence of these myths can stop people from seeking advice, support and diagnosis early, which will have an impact on the treatments available to them.

Dispelling myths – partnership care

CASE STUDY

Reflect back on Mr Crawthorne (see pages 204 and 206), who is now in residential care. Today his wife and grandchildren, aged 8 and 10, are visiting. They do come to visit on a regular basis but look awkward.

1. What possible myths and stereotypes may be responsible for the difficulties in Mr Crawthorne's relationship with his family?

How can you ease the tension?

2. Describe ways to develop a relationship with the family that will ease the tension you see on their visits and help to dispel myths.

3. Taking into account the personal history of Mr Crawthorne, what activities might you suggest for the family to do together?

Supporting ways to overcome fears and anxieties in individuals and carers

It is not uncommon for an individual with dementia and their family to be fearful and anxious about the future following their diagnosis. They will often look to you for guidance and reassurance, and there are a number of practical things you can do to reduce their anxiety and help them overcome their fears.

ACTIVITY

Providing information about local support groups is one way of supporting individuals to overcome their fears. Identify four other practical actions you can take to help an individual with dementia and their family to overcome their fears and anxieties.

✿

✿

✿

✿

Building on the last activity, there are other ways and means of accessing support that will be useful, not only for the family but for carers. They may also experience pressures and stress as they strive to be positive all the time.

Support agencies and benefits

ACTIVITY

Complete the table below to consider four agencies and how they might benefit the person, their family and the carer. You may wish to do some research on the internet. Of course, there are many more than four agencies, but think of ones that will serve the needs of the carers as well as the people. An example has been done for you.

Supporting agency	Example of a benefit for the person and their family	Example of a benefit for the carer
Alzheimer's Society.	Able to access specialised services.	Somewhere to turn to for support and information.

Muriel

CASE STUDY

Muriel has been living with dementia for four years now and is supported by a home carer so she can live in her own bungalow. Her family also support her needs. Recently, however, Muriel has become depressed, more forgetful and confused, less mobile and more agitated. She is finding it increasingly difficult to manage her meals, get dressed and attend to her toileting and hygiene.

1. What should the home carer do, and what actions have to be put in place?

2. What organisation or services should the carer contact?

3. What could be a possible reason for Muriel's depression and confusion, other than a worsening of the dementia?

Assessor tip

A good piece of evidence for your portfolio, and a way to demonstrate your knowledge and understanding, would be to create an information sheet about dementia that you could share with colleagues and/or carers.

ARE YOU READY FOR ASSESSMENT?

☑ **Do you know the following:**

☐ 1. The range of causes of dementia?

☐ 2. The types of memory impairment experienced by individuals with dementia?

☐ 3. The way that individuals process information and how this relates to the abilities and limitations of individuals with dementia?

☐ 4. The factors that can cause changes in an individual's condition that are not attributable to dementia?

☐ 5. The reasons for the fluctuations in the abilities and needs of an individual with dementia?

☐ 6. The impact of early diagnosis and follow-up to diagnosis on the individual and their family and friends?

☐ 7. The importance of following agreed ways of working when reporting and recording possible signs or symptoms of dementia?

☐ 8. The differences between person-centred and non-person-centred approaches to dementia care?

☐ 9. The different techniques that can be used to meet the fluctuating abilities and needs of an individual with dementia?

☐ 10. The myths and stereotypes related to dementia, and how they may affect the individual and their carers?

☐ 11. Ways to support individuals and their carers in overcoming their fears concerning their diagnosis of dementia?

UNIT HSC 3003

Provide support to maintain and develop skills for everyday life

This unit will help you to understand how individuals can be supported to lead an independent life, retaining or developing skills to manage everyday routines. You will be able to compare methods, agree a plan with an individual and consult others to support that plan within a partnership framework.

You will need to be able to:
* understand the context of supporting skills for everyday life
* support individuals to plan for maintaining and developing skills for everyday life
* support individuals to retain, regain or develop skills for everyday life
* evaluate support for developing or maintaining skills for everyday life.

Understand the context of supporting skills for everyday life

You will have learned from the previous units that it is very important to allow people choice, freedom of expression, dignity, privacy and the empowerment to make their own decisions and choices in life. This is important for their self-esteem and self-worth. If people do not have high self-esteem and self-worth, they may become apathetic, lose interest in life and looking after themselves, and eventually they could neglect hygiene and other basic needs.

Compare methods for developing and maintaining skills for everyday life

It used to be common practice for health care services to make decisions on behalf of people who needed support, such as those recovering from an operation or needing rehabilitation. Appointments would be made in outpatient departments, but the individual was not fully consulted. Research has shown, however, that when people are involved in their care and treatments, they tend to manage better and become independent more quickly. This method of working in partnership (which can involve family, friends and a range of health professionals) is called active participation.

Methods of managing care

THINK CASE STUDY

Mikhail is 69 and has returned home from hospital following a stroke, which has left him paralysed partially down his left side and with poor speech. Mikhail had the choice of either staying in a unit for rehabilitation for a further three weeks, or going home. Mikhail chose to come home, but he is able to access the facility on a day-to-day basis.

1. Why is it important for Mikhail to decide where he would like to be?

Mikhail has chosen to come home

2. Why is it important for the rehabilitation programme to be offered on a day-to-day basis?

3. What do you think are the overall benefits of Mikhail being cared for at home?

4. What other support may he need?

5. Give three examples of possible adaptations that could be made to Mikhail's home.

Reasons why individuals may need support to maintain, regain or develop skills for everyday life

What are the skills for everyday life? Think about how we use our bodies and our thinking and organising skills in this next activity.

ACTIVITY

Complete the table by ticking the appropriate columns to show which physical functions are needed for each everyday skill.

Skills for everyday life	Ability to mobilise (without aids)	Ability to see	Ability to hear (without the use of aids)	Ability to think, reason and organise	Ability to remember
Shopping.					
Making meals and drinks.					
Doing the laundry.					
Paying bills and managing money.					
Cleaning a house.					
Making telephone calls.					
Personal care.					

When you have completed the last activity, think about the problems that could arise when these functions or abilities break down. This could be because of an injury or the onset of a particular condition. You may have found that you have a lot of ticks for the columns in the previous activity, which should tell you that many everyday skills require our bodily systems to be integrated; those involving **cognitive skills** will also involve the **motor system**.

key terms

Cognitive skills: thinking and organising skills
Motor system: the skeletal and muscular system involved in movements.

Reasons for support

ACTIVITY

Look at this list of everyday skills that most people have to manage. In the table, explain which tasks will be difficult to do with the conditions listed in the first column and suggest some ways of supporting the tasks. Remember that it is likely the person will experience difficulty with more than one everyday skill. An example has been done for you.

Everyday skills

✿ Managing money and paying bills

✿ Managing medication

✿ Being sociable, by meeting or talking to friends and family

✿ Shopping

✿ Household chores and laundry

✿ Preparing and cooking meals

✿ Learning new skills

Condition	Everyday skills that will be difficult	Suggestions to support difficulties
Unable to walk.	Being sociable, by meeting or talking to friends and family.	The use of a wheelchair or walking frame will help.
Unable to see.		
Unable to organise thoughts.		
Acute depression.		
Learning difficulties.		

How maintaining, regaining or developing skills can benefit individuals

People who are recovering from an illness or an operation may feel vulnerable and weak. It is important to establish some independence as quickly as possible in order to benefit their self-esteem and overall well-being.

When people in hospital are getting ready for discharge, it is important to ensure that the individual is going home to some kind of care and support and a **needs analysis** is conducted.

Benefits

ACTIVITY

Imagine you have conducted a needs analysis on the people identified in column one. Identify the main problem areas in column two and suggest a solution in column three. Explain the benefits to overall health and well-being in column four. An example has been done for you.

The individual	Main problems	Example of a solution to regain or develop a new skill	Benefits to overall health and well-being
Mr A has sustained a back and leg injury, which will take a long time to recover from.	Mobility, perhaps using stairs and outside steps.	Using walking aids, such as crutches or a stick or frame.	The ability to mobilise and be more independent. Using muscles will be beneficial for circulation and general health.
Miss S has been dependent on drugs, which has left her anxious and afraid to go out.			
Mrs W has suffered a stroke that has resulted in **expressive dysphasia.**			
Mr T had retinal tears that have left him severely partially sighted.			

Be able to support individuals to plan for maintaining and developing skills for everyday life

In order to encourage active participation, it is necessary to ensure that the individual has the correct information to plan a positive way forward. Someone making transitions, such as following a stay in hospital or a specialised unit, may initially find some things difficult to manage. Returning to independent living can be a shock.

Working with an individual and others to identify support

Remember that active participation involves other people such as family, friends and health professionals. A plan will need the commitment and cooperation of others, as well as from the individual themselves.

Planning

ACTIVITY

You need to use some of your skills gathered from previous units, such as SHC 31 'Promote communication in health and social care settings' and HSC 036 'Promote person-centred care approaches in health and social care' to help you complete this activity.

Look at the skills given in column one and describe how you would do this in column two. Use column three to offer an example, using one of the individuals from the previous activity. An example has been done for you.

Care worker skill	How to do this	Example from previous activity
Active listening.	I would ensure that individuals express all their feelings, frustrations and wishes so that I can understand the situation, the issues involved and build a relationship based on trust.	I will find out how Mr T manages his everyday tasks, what he cannot do and what frustrates him.
Gathering a life history.		
Asking open questions.		

Care worker skill	How to do this	Example from previous activity
Involving others.		

When setting objectives or goals, remember to make them SMART, that is:

Specific – is it clear and understandable to everyone involved?

Measurable – how will everyone know what change/progress looks like?

Achievable – is it within the individual's capability?

Realistic – can it be achieved or are smaller steps required?

Timescale – how long will it take? When will we check progress?

If goals are SMART it will be easier to evaluate progress and for everyone to feel motivated by this.

Agree a plan

ACTIVITY

Reflect back on the skill of asking open questions 'covered in Unit HSC 036 'Promote person-centred approaches in health and social care' (see page 119). It is important that you ask the relevant questions in order to gather the necessary information. Look at the daily activities on the left and then complete the second column, giving two examples of questions you should ask. An example has been done for you.

Activity of daily living	Example of questions (What/When/Where/How?)
Personal care.	1. How do you manage to go to the toilet and get washed? 2. When do you normally take a bath or a shower?
Nutritional needs.	
Management of medications.	
Mobility around the home/ ability to complete chores.	

Activity of daily living	Example of questions (What/When/Where/How?)
Management of the outside and garden.	
Budgeting and paperwork.	
Socialising and leisure.	

Supporting the gaps in knowledge and skills

ACTIVITY

Read the information about the three individuals. For each person, identify what kind of knowledge and information they would need in order to manage their condition and suggest a relevant health professional to give guidance and support.

1. Before damaging his back and leg, **Mr A** enjoyed playing golf and managing a team of local youth footballers. You discover that his current lack of exercise and mobility may be a bigger problem as before his accident exercise was part of his life.

   ✿ What knowledge will benefit Mr A?

   ✿ What health professional or organisation may be able to support his lack of mobility?

   ✿ If no support plan was in place, what might happen to Mr A?

2. **Miss S** was a dancer before becoming dependent on drugs to keep her awake and full of energy. She fears she has no other skills to use and will lose her dancing ability as well.

❀ What knowledge will help Miss S?

❀ What health professional or organisation can be consulted?

❀ What might happen if Miss S was not supported?

3. **Mr T** is 76 years old and has loved to read all his life, but since his retinal tears he has been unable to read his books or tend to his plants properly in the garden. He also fears that he will not be able to manage his bills or read his correspondence. Shopping is no longer a pleasure as he is unable to see things properly.

❀ What knowledge will help Mr T?

❀ What health professional or organisation will be useful to him?

❀ What might happen to Mr T if no support was given?

I said not from the market!

The possible sources of conflict and how to resolve them

Health professionals, friends and family may be very keen to help, but there are often obstacles that can stand in the way of a plan's success. Friends and relatives also have their own commitments and often their support is voluntary. Support may be very willingly offered at first but may lessen as commitments in their own lives get in the way. Another possible conflict is a poor relationship between the individual and the person helping them. If this is the case, the individual may not want to follow suggestions, may refuse ideas in the plan, or accept them but not actually do them.

Possible conflicts

ACTIVITY

Look at the plan that Mr T has decided on and agreed to. Think carefully about his comments and requests and identify the potential conflicts. Think of a positive and constructive solution if a conflict arises. An example has been done for you.

Daily activity	Plan	Possible conflict	Possible solution
Personal care.	Can see to this himself, as long as his daughter and daughter-in-law leave out his clothes, soap, shaving foam and plentiful clean towels.	Conflicts may arise if his daughter or daughter-in-law do not keep his clothes in the same place or his shaving foam is not topped up.	A solution may be to help him to arrange his shaving foam and clothes by labelling a drawer and marking containers with brightly coloured stickers.
Shopping.	Agrees to give lists to daughter-in-law but only likes certain brands.		
Laundry and cleaning.	Daughter sees to laundry and cleaning the house twice a week. But she has her own job, house and family to attend to so may miss a day.		
Leisure.	Daughter will take him out in the car for fresh air twice a week but again may not manage this all the time.		

Daily activity	Plan	Possible conflict	Possible solution
Managing medication.	Agreed to receive a NOMAD system but some tablets will only be taken when necessary and Mr T cannot read their labels. He does not understand why he has to take so many pills and refuses those that he cannot swallow.		

Supporting individuals to understand the processes, procedures and equipment that are needed to implement and monitor plans

All aspects of a plan need to be understood and appreciated. For example, the reasons for taking medication should be understood by the individual. If full information is given, they have a choice: they will know what the possible outcomes of participating in or not accepting treatments may be.

Full understanding

ACTIVITY

Whatever the disability or condition that an individual has to live with, there are always some ways to work with the strengths of that person and develop skills and knowledge so that they can cope reasonably well.

Read the following 'desirable targets' of individuals who have recently been discharged from institutional care and suggest training to help them to regain or develop new coping skills. List any equipment that might assist this process. An example has been done for you.

Individual	Desirable target	Suggested training/procedures	Possible equipment
Michael has to manage his new diagnosis of being an insulin-dependent diabetic.	To manage my diet and condition without feeling unwell, and to inject myself when I need to.	To teach Michael how to inject himself and dispose of the needles safely. Education involves knowing about diabetes and blood sugar levels and how to manage his diet.	Needles for subcutaneous injections and sharps boxes (for disposal). Equipment to measure his blood sugar levels and a diet plan.
Bill has been discharged following major heart surgery but is anxious and apprehensive about exercising.	To enjoy walks and outings without exertion or feeling dizzy or breathless.		

Individual	Desirable target	Suggested training/procedures	Possible equipment
Mrs Powley was hospitalised following a flare up of her MS (multiple sclerosis).	To get around the house and garden without using my wheelchair.		

Whatever your ideas, you will need to monitor them to check that they are working and ask the individual at regular and agreed times what issues have arisen, what works for them and what doesn't.

Assessor tip

Ask one of the service users you act as a key worker for if your assessor can attend their care planning meeting, so that they can observe you. Make sure other people involved are also aware of your assessor being present. Remind them that your assessor is bound by confidentiality, just as you are.

Support individuals to retain, regain or develop skills for everyday life

So far we have looked at people's skills in the home for managing everyday life. However, some people you care for would have been working, and for them the loss of employment may be devastating.

Provide support to develop or maintain skills

ACTIVITY

Remember not to lose sight of the need to involve the person in active participation.

Read the cases below and summarise what you might offer in the way of learning a new skill to find employment. State who you might contact to support these people further and suggest what other support may be needed to facilitate a productive working life.

1. Tony, aged 48, is now a wheelchair user following an accident. He can no longer continue with his manual job. He likes photography and gardening.

2. Henry, aged 52, has chronic obstructive pulmonary disease (COPD). He has learned to live with his condition and is willing to work but soon gets tired. He likes meeting people, being in his garden and doing word puzzles.

3. Mrs Graham has three small children and her husband works away from home. She has suffered from acute panic attacks. She wants to work again, but not in crowded noisy environments.

Giving positive and constructive feedback

No matter what your personal circumstances are, everyone has days when we don't feel our best and everyday life seems difficult to get through. We all appreciate positive feedback, and when we struggle we need constructive comments and actions that encourage us. It is exactly the same for the people you care for.

Positive feedback

ACTIVITY

Read the progress reports for some of the individuals mentioned in this unit. Remind yourself of their cases again by re-reading the earlier activities.

What would you say to them that would be positive and constructive?

Individual's progress	Your positive and constructive feedback
Miss S has managed two rides on the bus to town but tells you she was shaking when walking to the bus stop.	

Individual's progress	Your positive and constructive feedback
Tony (a wheelchair user) is enjoying his new photography training course but the equipment he needs at times is stored on high shelves.	
Mrs Graham has fewer panic attacks since getting out and starting a job. However, she is struggling to keep her three children and the house as clean and tidy as she likes.	

What actions can be taken if an individual becomes distressed or unable to cope?

Sometimes an individual may not want to continue with plans that enable independence. This may be a temporary measure or it may be permanent if the person becomes too ill, too weak or frightened to do things on their own.

You must carry on supporting them, but the methods may change and the health care professionals will also change according to the support needed.

ACTIVITY

Working to regain, develop or maintain everyday skills as a result of an accident or illness can be hard for individuals to bear. It is important to understand the reasons why people may become distressed so that you can support them.

Identify three reasons why an individual may become distressed and how you could support them.

✿

✿

Joint efforts

ACTIVITY

Read the following short case histories and answer the questions.

1. Maisie was confined to her house after having a hip replacement and has been managing well, but when venturing out into town she fell over and now her confidence is lost.

   Describe the actions of a visiting team to support her to regain her confidence.

2. Arthur, aged 92, has managed independent living with the help and support of his daughter and son and their families. But recently his son died, leaving Arthur depressed, with little interest in his life.

   Describe three steps a health care team can take to support Arthur.

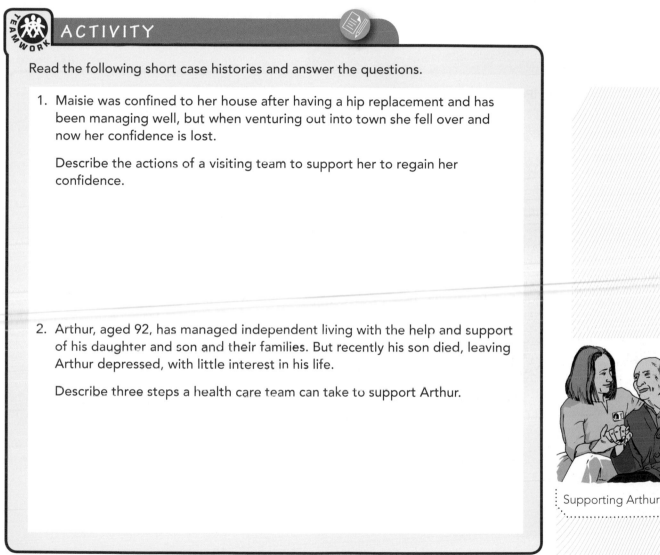

Supporting Arthur

Evaluate support for developing or maintaining skills for everyday life

It is important to agree with an individual about what is working and what needs changing. Individuals will have an idea of what they can realistically do with support. This needs to be identified so that a team can evaluate whether or not this has been achieved and what still needs to be done if not.

Work with an individual to agree criteria and processes for evaluating support

An individual's goals are one aspect to address but it is also important to consider the methods needed to enable the person to maintain or develop skills. Timescales are important to help evaluate progress. Any progress could deteriorate if you leave discussions too late. You have to agree goals, methods and timescales with the individual, the family and others, and agree to modify plans if they are not enabling progress.

Evaluate progress towards goals and record in line with agreed ways of working

ACTIVITY

Read again the activity 'Positive feedback' (page 229), which gave you the task of giving positive and encouraging feedback to individuals. This activity gives you the opportunity to think about how you might support that positive feedback.

Complete the following table with your ideas of what the individual's personal goal or target might be, your methods to support this, what the agreed timescales might be and the possible revised targets and additional support methods.

Individual's progress	Personal goal and how to support this	Agreed timescales	Revised targets and additional support methods
Miss S has managed two rides on the bus to town but tells you she was shaking when walking to the bus stop.			
Tony (a wheelchair user) is enjoying his new photography training course but the equipment he needs at times is stored on high shelves.			

Individual's progress	Personal goal and how to support this	Agreed timescales	Revised targets and additional support methods
Mrs Graham has fewer panic attacks since getting out and starting a job. However, she is struggling to keep her three children and the house as clean and tidy as she likes.			

Your questions answered...

How can I best support someone to live independently again after a long time in care?

Use the principles of planning, such as actively listening to the needs of that person and identifying what aspects need to be supported and how. This will take some considerable time, especially at an initial interview. It is crucial to establish what the person is capable of doing, confident at doing and able to do with support. You must ask the right questions to determine how the individual feels. Being cared for in an institution is very different from caring for oneself. An assessment of needs is essential, ensuring avenues of support are in place and that follow-up reviews are conducted in a timely manner.

Assessor tip

If your assessor is unable to directly observe you undertaking an evaluation of progress, use work records and witness testimony to demonstrate and confirm your competence. You can also use the care plan as a basis for discussion.

Mr T

CASE STUDY

Mr T was experiencing issues with the care support provided by his daughter and daughter-in-law. Some suggestions were made to deal with potential conflict issues, and it is now necessary to evaluate how that support from the family and others is being sustained alongside Mr T's self-care management.

Francesca, his carer, arrives to review the plan, which seems positive, except that Mr T's days out have now stopped because his daughter has increased her hours of work. However, as Francesca looks around the house, she notices it is not as clean as it once was and Mr T does not want her in the kitchen.

He appears thinner and when Francesca asks about his meals, he laughs and says he has no appetite and she is not to worry.

1. How would you best establish the problems he is experiencing but perhaps not sharing?

2. What needs to be revised in terms of the original plan? (See the 'Possible conflicts' activity on page 229.)

3. What would you suggest to resolve the suspected support gaps?

4. Why do you think Francesca needs to be sensitive with this issue?

5. What are the risks involved?

6. What information should Francesca pass on to her manager in line with agreed ways of working?

ARE YOU READY FOR ASSESSMENT?

☑ **Do you know the following:**

☐ 1. How to compare different methods for supporting individuals to develop and maintain everyday skills?

☐ 2. The reasons why individuals may require support to maintain, regain or develop everyday living skills?

☐ 3. The benefits to the individual of maintaining, regaining and developing everyday skills?

☐ 4. The possible sources of conflict when planning, and ways to resolve them?

☐ 5. The actions to take if an individual becomes distressed or is unable to continue an activity?

☑ **Can you do the following:**

☐ 1. Work with individuals to identify the everyday living skills they need to develop?

☐ 2. Agree a plan with the individual for developing or maintaining their everyday living skills?

☐ 3. Support the individual in understanding the plan and any processes, procedures or equipment that may be needed to implement it?

☐ 4. Promote active participation when providing agreed support to develop or maintain skills?

☐ 5. Give the individual positive and constructive feedback during activities relating to developing or maintaining everyday skills?

☐ 6. Agree criteria for evaluating the support given to an individual, with them and others involved?

☐ 7. Evaluate the individual's progress towards goals and the effectiveness of methods used according to your agreed role?

☐ 8. Agree revisions to the plan?

☐ 9. Record and report progress and outcomes according to agreed ways of working?

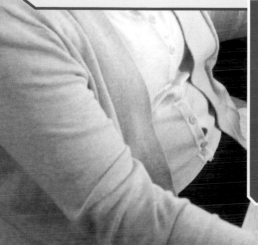

UNIT HSC 3013

Support individuals to access and use services and facilities

This unit will help you to understand factors that influence access to services and facilities, the barriers to access and how these may be overcome. It also examines how to work with individuals to identify access, make use of, and sustain, services and the use of facilities.

You will need to be able to:

✿ understand factors that influence individuals' access to services and facilities

✿ support individuals to select services and facilities

✿ support individuals to access and use services and facilities

✿ support individuals to review their access to, and use of, services and facilities.

Factors that influence individuals' access to services and facilities

How accessing a range of services can be beneficial

The move away from institutionalised care has meant that home care and community facilities have had to improve. People generally want to stay in their own homes and be near their friends and families, and this factor alone is a benefit to their well-being and self-esteem.

Allied health professionals are specialists in various areas and are able to assist with community care services. Voluntary and community services also offer a range of services to help people get back into work or manage a better standard of living and overall health and well-being.

Benefitting individual situations

ACTIVITY

Look at the people in the first column and briefly describe the services that you think can benefit their situations. Remember that suggestions can be rejected or modified to be reviewed later. An example has been done for you.

The individual and the circumstances	Voluntary and community services	Home care services (social care and respite)	Condition-specific information	Financial support	Rehabilitation services
Linda is a 66-year-old carer of a son aged 40 with complex needs. Her husband has recently died and she is finding it difficult to cope.	Luncheon clubs and voluntary support.	Short- and long-term respite care. Social care and home care services.	May not be required as she has looked after her son for 40 years.	Help in accessing respite care. Being able to take a break.	Not necessary.
Eleanor is a Caribbean woman living alone. She has just been diagnosed with diabetes and is afraid of how this will affect her health and lifestyle.					

The individual and the circumstances	Voluntary and community services	Home care services (social care and respite)	Condition-specific information	Financial support	Rehabilitation services
Cath is a divorced 56-year-old company director. She has sustained loss of vision and has been diagnosed 'severely partially sighted'.					
Rafael, aged 42, is an engineer. He has just suffered a heart attack, and fears how this will impact his work and spoil his sporting pursuits of golf and tennis.					

Barriers that individuals may encounter in accessing services and facilities

So what might stop individuals from accessing services and facilities? What might be a barrier?

Possible barriers

  ACTIVITY

Look at the table below, which lists some disabling conditions or factors. In the second column list what might be a reason for not accessing services and facilities, and in the third column briefly list ways to overcome these barriers. An example has been done for you.

Condition or factor	Possible barriers	Possible solutions
Hearing impairment.	Lack of confidence.	Hearing services in the home given by visiting professionals.
Visual impairment.		

Condition or factor	Possible barriers	Possible solutions
Poor mobility.		
Panic attacks.		
Living in a rural or difficult-to-reach area.		

Information barriers

ACTIVITY

The table below lists some communication scenarios in the first column. Use the second column to identify possible faults and barriers with these scenarios. You could consider the disabling conditions in the previous activity and a range of different types of people. Then describe possible solutions to these barriers in the third column. An example has been done for you.

Communication scenario	Barriers that may arise	Possible solutions
Visiting an outpatient department.	Reading and understanding letters about appointments.	Care worker or family member to read letter and ensure individual understands it.
Making a phone call to a hospital or clinic.		
Completing a form.		
Going online.		

Support individuals to challenge information about services that may present a barrier to participation

Participation in services requires understanding of the information given and the individual's consent. Consent cannot be given if people do not understand the information they receive or cannot access it in the first place.

I don't understand!

ACTIVITY

Read the difficulties that these individuals are experiencing. Explain what support and advice you would give to them if they complained to you while you were making a visit.

1. Mr Khan has received a letter from the outpatients department of a large hospital that he says is too long and that his English is not good enough to translate.

2. Mrs O'Gormon has made several phone calls to the local environmental health department because she has seen mice in her flat. She tells you that 'the woman' keeps asking her to press different numbers and she gets nowhere.

3. Miss Bartlett would like information about her condition, but when calling a support society she is told that all information is now online and no more paper leaflets will be published 'to protect the environment'. She asks you how she can read this information without a computer.

Support individuals to select services and facilities

Individuals will usually welcome the opportunity to find out about the services and facilities that can help them to be in better health and enjoy independence and improved well-being. Professionals are often more knowledgeable and in a better position to have access to this information than individuals; however, it is important for individuals to try to discover for themselves the services, facilities and equipment that will work best for them.

Reflect on the assessment of needs and a needs analysis to identify the kind of support that a person will require. Remember also 'active participation' when the person is in control of the plan, in partnership with others (see page 222).

Day care or homecare?

Identify services and facilities

ACTIVITY

Day care can be offered on a regular basis (Monday to Friday) or for just one or two days a week. Some people do not wish to go to a day care centre but prefer to stay at home.

Read the list of some adult day care services in the first column. What options can you think of for providing the same services at home? Write your answers in the second column and comment on whether you think the service would be better suited to the day care centre, the home or both. An example has been done for you.

Adult day care services	Alternative home care?
Meals are offered.	Meals provided by Social Services (some home carers) and private providers. This would be suitable for both so would be the individual's choice.
Medical consultations.	

Adult day care services	Alternative home care?
Physical exercise and therapy.	
Socialisation.	
Health screening.	
Education and training.	
Counselling.	
Chiropody.	

Selecting services and facilities

ACTIVITY

Read the list of support needs in the first column and use the second column to identify a range of services and equipment that might help. Research how to access these and use the third column to indicate a relevant organisation and describe how it can support these particular needs. An example has been done for you.

Assessed support need	Examples of service/equipment/ assisted technology	Contact organisation
Assistance with mobility in the house and the garden.	Chairlifts, hand-rails on the stairs and in the garden. Ramps where there are restrictive steps. Adaptation of the sleeping arrangements – perhaps moving the bed to a downstairs room. Installing a downstairs toilet. Adapting the height of appliances for easier use.	Social Services and the local authority may provide grants for modifications. Private companies will sell some chairlifts and gardening services.

Assessed support need	Examples of service/equipment/ assisted technology	Contact organisation
Assistance with vision – difficulties using electrical appliances, shopping (reading labels), cooking and paying bills.		
Assistance with personal care – difficulties getting in and out of a bath.		
Anxiety and social isolation – depression and poor motivation.		
A computer programmer has suffered a stroke, disabling the right hand.		
Man has been made redundant in his early 50s, so needs to retrain.		

Health services

ACTIVITY

This activity is similar to the previous one, except that this covers health and medical needs that require a service or facility.

Read the medical issues and complete this table. An example has been done for you.

Medical need	Examples of service and/or equipment	Contact organisation
Unable to see medication labels or identify tablets.	Large print labels (can be used for painkillers that do not need to be taken all the time). A NOMAD system for regular medication.	GP and pharmacist, for ways to provide the medications required and to find out if the local pharmacist will deliver, if required.

Medical need	Examples of service and/or equipment	Contact organisation
Person with diabetes is unable to stabilise blood sugar levels.		
Ulcerating skin condition requires dressings.		
Unable to cope since a recent bereavement.		
Need to build up strength and stamina following heart surgery.		

Home services

ACTIVITY

This activity looks at needs within the home that may require a service or facility. Read the home care issues that may arise and complete the table.

Home care need	Examples of service	Contact organisation
Help with gardening.		

Home care need	Examples of service	Contact organisation
Household chores.		
Finances and paperwork.		

Support individuals to access and use services and facilities

Once you have helped the individual to identify a service, you will need to ensure they know how to use the services or equipment to get the maximum benefit. It is important to agree methods of support and times of attendance at any facility, as well as the timescales for reviewing services and facilities in the future.

Identify with an individual the resources, support and assistance required

ACTIVITY

Read the following snapshots of people who have agreed to a service.

1. Mr Chauhan has agreed to visit a gym following heart surgery, to build up strength and stamina with a personal trainer.

   How will you support him? What information will you give him?

2. Abida was a cook in Egypt and now, although she speaks little English, she would like to train for a career in preparing food.

   What organisation can help Abida? What support will she need?

3. Mrs Dovbenko has fallen over because of poor vision and unsteadiness on her feet. She sleeps upstairs but would like an additional handrail. She has been sent a long and complicated form to complete to assess whether she is eligible for funding.

   What will you ensure is highlighted clearly on the form, so that Mrs Dovbenko has the best chances for receiving financial support?

ACTIVITY

When supporting individuals to access and use services and facilities, there are a number of factors that need to be considered to establish the level of support they may require.

Identify four factors that you should consider when deciding on the level of support that an individual would require.

✿

✿

✿

✿

Agree responsibilities to enable the individual to access and use services and facilities

Much depends on the type of service or equipment being accessed, but there are certain responsibilities that the individual must consider. Places at day care centres are sometimes limited and people may be on a waiting list. If services are focused on regular visits the person should be at home when the care worker arrives. Appointments with health professionals should be kept, as valuable time will have been wasted that could have been used working with another person.

Responsibilities

key terms

Community psychiatric nurse: a visiting health professional who gives support to people with mental health issues.
Aseptically: a process for cleaning and re-dressing wounds that uses a non-touch technique and a sterile field.

Individual's legal rights for accessing services and facilities

Individuals wanting to access services and equipment to help them achieve improved health and well-being have every right to do so without experiencing discrimination.

Under the **Equality Act 2010**, individuals have rights of access to employment opportunities, education and training, goods, services and facilities and financial rights to buy or rent property.

Under the **Human Rights Act 1998**, individuals have a right to be respected, be treated as an individual, be protected from harm or danger, cared for in ways that they choose, access information about themselves and communicate in their preferred language.

Within a health and social care context you are expected to maintain a duty of care (see SHC 34 'Principles for implementing duty of care') and work within a framework of standards and codes of practice.

Rights and standards

ACTIVITY

Tick the following statements to indicate whether you think they are true or false.

TRUE/FALSE

- ✿ An individual has a right to free transport to a hospital, clinic or day centre.
- ✿ It is a legal duty for public buildings to provide ramps for access.
- ✿ An employer has a duty to accommodate and support the health needs of employees.
- ✿ Social Services must install chairlifts free of charge.
- ✿ An individual can qualify for a grant to support home modifications.
- ✿ Proposed activities and services must be risk assessed.
- ✿ The individual's decision for services is always upheld with no further risk assessments.

Support individuals to review their access to, and use of, services and facilities

Work with individuals to evaluate services

ACTIVITY

When an individual is finding a service or active participation difficult, they may want to make changes but they may not readily say this to you. In this activity, imagine that you are visiting the following individuals in a community care setting. When you ask how they are feeling, they describe certain aspects of support as given below. What will you report to your line manager? Summarise this in the second column.

The individual's review statement	What you will record and report
Tracey says: 'I have been Tom's carer for 18 years and, although I am his mother, I cannot do this all the time by myself any more. He is too heavy for me to lift and I am getting a very bad back. The help I get is too little.'	
Mrs Hall says: 'The day centre is good in some ways but the people are very noisy. I do like their trips out into the country but if I don't go every week I may lose my place.'	

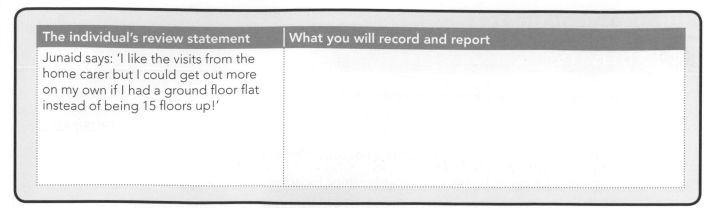

The individual's review statement	What you will record and report
Junaid says: 'I like the visits from the home carer but I could get out more on my own if I had a ground floor flat instead of being 15 floors up!'	

Assessor tip

Arrange for your assessor to accompany you and a service user on an activity where you access services and facilities in the community. This would be a good opportunity to demonstrate a wide range of knowledge and skills.

Part of your role in supporting individuals to access and use services and facilities is to support them in providing feedback on these. It is important that individuals are given the opportunity to comment on services and facilities. The service or facility may have a formal feedback process, such as a written questionnaire, or an informal process where the individual can make their comments verbally to a member of staff. Remember, feedback is the means by which improvements can be made, so it is important both for individuals working in the service as well as those using it.

Evaluating services and facilities

In order to evaluate something you need a starting base. The initial assessment of needs or needs analysis will have given you this. The individual will, hopefully, have made progress once they started to use services or facilities, but to fully evaluate the progress you will need to ask questions and invite feedback. Part of this evaluation will be to focus on the individual before accessing the services and after using the services.

ACTIVITY

Look at the issues involved in accessing services and facilities in the first column.

Decide on two questions you would ask to evaluate that approach; one should be about the person and one about the facility or service. Write these in the second column. An example has been done for you.

Service facility accessed	Questions to evaluate success
Attending group sessions for the visually impaired.	1. Do you enjoy going to the sessions? 2.
Attending computer training.	1. 2.
Using an adapted leg prosthesis.	1. 2.

Service facility accessed	Questions to evaluate success
Coping with a guide dog.	1.
	2.

If the individual's care plan has SMART (Specific, Measurable, Achievable, Realistic and have Timescales) objectives or goals, it will be easier to evaluate as the measures for success and change are clearly described (see Unit HSC 3003 'Provide support to maintain and develop skills' for information on setting SMART objectives or goals).

ACTIVITY

Think about the care plan goals or objectives for an individual you support in relation to accessing and using services and facilities.

Write SMART goals for the individual.

Identify and agree any changes needed to improve the experience and outcomes of using services or facilities

Some changes that are needed may just relate to small things, such as having medications delivered by the local pharmacist and placed in a NOMAD system, or a neighbour, relative or friend with a car fetching large items from a supermarket.

The following case study gives you the opportunity to think about the changes that may affect individuals' lives to a larger extent and, that therefore, will need closer and more frequent monitoring.

Assessor tip

Evaluating the success of using services and facilities can happen after each use and not just after the time specified in the care plan. For example, your assessor can observe you getting feedback from the individual after an activity and then discuss with you how you will use this to inform future activities.

251

Mr Abrahams

CASE STUDY

Mr Abrahams lives with his son and daughter-in-law. He attends an adult day care centre three days a week while his daughter-in-law works. His son collects him. He thought it was all right initially, but the activities on offer were jigsaws and bingo, neither of which interests him. In fact he enjoys his own company, using the computer and reading. He can walk unaided but is rather unsteady on his legs when tired.

At home, his son and daughter-in-law cook his evening meal, and do his shopping and laundry. However, soon his son's job will be relocated 150 miles away for a one-year contract. His daughter-in-law will move with her husband.

Mr Abrahams has been offered a full-time place (Monday to Friday) at the centre but his accommodation now has to be changed. The plan is for him to live in sheltered housing.

Mr Abrahams enjoys reading

1. What questions do you think Mr Abrahams will ask about the change in his support network?

2. Research the facility of 'sheltered housing' in terms of provision and the staff responsibilities. What are your findings?

3. Evaluate the benefits that you think Mr Abrahams may experience and the issues that you will need to review.

ARE YOU READY FOR ASSESSMENT?

☑ **Do you know the following:**

☐ 1. The benefits to individuals of accessing different services and facilities?

☐ 2. The barriers that individuals may have to accessing services and facilities, and how to overcome them?

☐ 3. The reasons why it is important to support individuals to challenge information about services that may be a barrier to their participation?

☐ 4. How to promote individuals' rights and preferences when they access and use services and facilities?

☐ 5. How to identify and agree any changes needed to improve the individual's experience and outcomes of accessing and using services and facilities?

☑ **Can you do the following:**

☐ 1. Work with an individual to identify and select a range of services and facilities that meet their assessed needs?

☐ 2. Agree the individual's preferred options for accessing services and facilities?

☐ 3. Identify with an individual the resources, support and assistance they will need to access and use the services and facilities they have selected?

☐ 4. Enable individuals to access and use services and facilities within the scope of your role and responsibilities?

☐ 5. Evaluate, with the individual, whether services and facilities have met their assessed needs?

☐ 6. Support individuals in providing feedback to others on their experience of accessing and using services and facilities?

☐ 7. Evaluate, with the individual, the support provided to access services and facilities?

Glossary

ACAS: the Advisory, Conciliation and Arbitration Service. www.acas.org.uk.

Active participation: this is when individuals are fully involved in all aspects of care and treatments, taking part in activities that they wish to, and agreeing activities in partnership with others.

Advocate: someone who speaks on another person's behalf.

Agency: an organisation that provides a particular service.

Allege: to declare or assert.

Argyle's theory of the communication cycle: a theory suggesting that ideas are communicated, acted upon and reviewed. There are six stages but the hardest is the 'decoding' stage because that is when our messages are understood or misunderstood by others.

Aseptically: a process for cleaning and re-dressing wounds that uses a non-touch technique and a sterile field.

Audit trail: evidence of good standards observed by examining records.

Barrier nursing: nursing a patient who might be infectious to others, or protecting a patient from infections that would harm them.

Barriers: anything that blocks the positive attitudes needed in society to value individuals.

Barriers to effective communication: anything that hinders effective communication, such as language, hearing impairments, visual impairments, inappropriate vocabulary, excessive background noise or poor lighting.

Behavioural signs: examples might be crying, being withdrawn and miserable or even antisocial and aggressive behaviour.

Best interests: decisions that are based on the most appropriate care or treatment for that person.

Body language: the way we use our bodies to indicate or express the way we feel.

Codes of practice: a set of agreed behaviours that adhere to professional standards.

Cognitive signs: cognition relates to thinking and reasoning. If we are depressed, our thoughts are negative and sometimes irrational. We may also find it difficult to concentrate and apply ourselves to thinking tasks. This can be damaging to us and others through the behavioural signs.

Cognitive skills: thinking and organising skills.

Common Induction Standards: a set of eight standards (mapped across the diploma) that form the induction process into the care sector.

Common law of confidentiality: a common understanding that the information you pass on to a doctor, for example, will be kept confidential.

Community psychiatric nurse: a visiting health professional who gives support to people with mental health issues.

Complex needs: where there is a combination of factors that contribute to poor health and well-being.

Confidentiality: ensuring that information is accessible only to those authorised to have access.

CPR: Cardio-pulmonary resuscitation is the recognised artificial resuscitation procedure following a cardiac arrest, possibly as a result of a heart attack.

Cross-contamination: this is when a contaminated source or object has come into contact with another source, for example when unwashed hands touch vulnerable service users.

Cue: any sign or body language that conveys the feelings of others. In the health and social care sector it is very important to respond to cues appropriately.

Discrimination: actions or attitudes that treat other people less favourably.

Diversity: differences between individuals and groups, for example culture, race, gender, religion, age, abilities and disabilities, sexual orientation and social class.

Duty of care: a legal obligation to work by set standards, as far as it is reasonable to do so, in order to prevent any harm or danger to those in your care.

Effective communication: any method of communication that achieves the desired result, that is, so the individual can understand and express needs or respond correctly to instructions.

Empowered: this is when an individual feels stronger, more confident or powerful owing to having more control over their life.

Equality: dignity, respect and rights for all individuals, whatever their differences.

Essential Standards of Quality and Safety: a set of 16 regulations, each with an identified outcome that is used to measure the standards of care providers.

Evaluate: to examine something in order to judge its value, quality, importance and the degree to which it applies. Evaluation always concludes with a judgement or recommendation.

Expressive dysphasia: the inability to express thoughts and feelings clearly in words.

Gesture: any bodily movement, such as waving arms, wagging fingers or shaking of the head, to indicate a particular feeling.

Hazard: the presence of anything that can cause actual harm.

Health and safety representative: an employee who oversees all health and safety issues and is an advocate for the staff, patients and residents. They are entitled to be given sufficient time to perform their duties.

Holistic care package: a combination of services put together to meet all of a person's needs.

Holistic health: a perspective that views the person as a whole, considering social, physical, intellectual, communication and emotional needs. General health and well-being are improved when all needs are met.

Identity: the characteristics that make you who you are.

Inclusion: individuals are included in services and provisions that reflect their different requirements for care and education and enable a sense of being valued.

Inclusive practice: this ensures that all individuals are valued and services are centred on each individual's needs and requirements.

Individuality: the personal aspects that make each individual unique. It often involves a history, for example a farmer who gets up very early will probably continue to be an early riser when he or she retires. Personalisation will allow for that.

Medical model of disability: this model seeks to 'cure' rather than adapt. The person with the disability is seen as a problem, rather than the barriers that prevent their requirements being met (for example, steps preventing a wheelchair user from entering a building).

Motor system: the skeletal and muscular system involved in movements.

Multi-agency working: where a number of different agencies work together with a common goal.

Multidisciplinary meeting: this brings together people with different roles and specialities who have the same aims, for example to provide care and support.

Musculoskeletal disorders: injury to muscles and bones, particularly in joints and the back.

National Minimum Standards: (for good quality care) a comprehensive range of responsibilities.

National Occupational Standards: a set of standards devised to inform and expect good practice in health and social care settings. Also used to develop qualifications and inform recruitment initiatives.

Needs analysis: a method of identifying how an individual manages the skills of everyday life. Based on a set of questions, it analyses the type of help needed to maintain independence.

Neutral: unbiased, not taking sides.

Non-verbal communication (NVC): conveying a feeling or a message without saying the actual words.

Objective: what you see and hear, not what you assume to be the meaning, which is deemed to exist only in your mind (subjective).

Open questions: these offer the opportunity to expand on the answer, for example by using 'How?', 'What?', 'Where?' 'When?' and give you more information, as opposed to closed questions that people can answer with just 'yes' or 'no'.

Partnership working: where professionals from different departments or organisations come together to use their expertise to best help and support individuals.

Passive: inactive, dependent on others, unwilling to make decisions and choices.

Passive recipient: the person is subject to others' ideas of what will benefit them rather than being consulted.

Pathogenic bacteria: bacteria that are harmful and can make us ill.

Perpetrator: someone who carries out abuse.

Person-centred care approach: this explores the likes, dislikes and preferences of each individual and ensures they have choice and control over their lives.

Personalisation: ensuring that the person is consulted on a full range of care issues and an agreed regime fits in with the person's wishes.

Physical environment: this considers the outside space as well as the rooms inside, such as a personal room, a communal room, bathrooms and toilets (which nowadays are mostly en-suite).

Physical signs and complaints: headaches, stomach problems and general tiredness are examples of physical signs that relate to feelings of stress.

Potential dilemma: a situation that may make you question your practice because an individual's choices and decisions may conflict with your own views.

PPE: personal protective equipment, for example a uniform, hats, gloves and aprons that create a barrier between the wearer and the vulnerable person or contaminated substance.

Prejudice: an opinion formed without real or sufficient knowledge and understanding. It is based on inaccurate information, irrational feelings, stereotypes, labels and assumptions, with no consideration of the individual.

Processing of data: obtaining, recording, holding, altering, retrieving and destroying or disclosing data or information.

Professional boundaries: limits that tell you what you can and can't do in your job role.

Receptive dysphasia: failing to understand the spoken word.

Reflective practice: analysing the way you behave or think about situations. It can refer to thinking during or after an event. It is usually considered as a tool to develop improved ways of working.

Risk assessment: the process of identifying hazards in the workplace, assessing the risks in terms of the harm they might cause, evaluating how best to reduce the risks and monitoring and reviewing actions taken.

Risks: the possibility of suffering harm or being exposed to danger.

Self-directed support: working in partnership with health professionals to manage self care with identified support strategies.

Self-esteem: a way of feeling about oneself that can be positive or negative depending on how a person perceives their identity and self-image. Low self-esteem can potentially affect health and well-being.

Self-fulfilling prophecy: one's belief in others' perceptions, often viewed as a negative belief.

Self-image: how you perceive yourself – your impression of who you are.

Sensitive issue: an issue that raises potential disagreements with the accepted care regimes and means that risks may be taken to balance benefits for individuals.

Setting: a place where people receive care and support, such as a hospital ward or their own home.

Social model of disability: including society in addressing issues of disability in a positive way, for example everyone being able to use sign language so they can communicate with the minority who use sign language.

Standard precautions: practices such as wearing PPE and effective hand washing. If everyone practised these precautions, the risk of infections spreading would be reduced as far as it is reasonably possible to do so.

Stereotype: perceiving people as a certain type, according to how they dress or behave.

Strengths-based approach: delivering care to focus on the strengths and positive activities that the person is able to do, not what they are unable to do.

Stressors: anything that causes stress.

Subcutaneous injection: an injection that is given just under the skin into the subcutaneous tissue. An example is heparin or insulin. Care workers can be trained to give these injections.

Tangible evidence: evidence that can be seen, measured or examined.

Task orientated: being focused on the jobs that need to be done rather than the person. This is the opposite approach to person-centred care.

Tuckman's theory of group formation: a theory suggesting that teams develop in stages. This is the forming of a team, the storming process (such as discussions and plans), norming (plans are being put into place) and performing (the team works together).

Visual, auditory and kinaesthetic: this refers respectively to seeing or watching, listening, and doing things, such as exploring or experimenting (kinaesthetic).

Vulnerable group: babies, young children, older people and adults with weak immune systems are more susceptible to disease and illness caused by pathogenic bacteria.

Whistle-blower: someone who tells the public or someone in authority about alleged or illegal activities taking place in their workplace.